DESIGNING
FOR INDUSTRY

DESIGNING
FOR INDUSTRY

THE
ARCHITECTURE OF
ALBERT KAHN

The MIT Press
Cambridge, Massachusetts
and London, England

Grant Hildebrand

Albert Kahn, Henry Ford,
Glenn Martin, and Charles Sorensen.
(Photograph by Joseph Klima,
courtesy of Mrs. Barnett Malbin.)

Copyright © 1974 by
The Massachusetts Institute of Technology

This book was set in CRT Baskerville and printed by Murray Printing Co. and bound by Colonial Press in the
United States of America.

Library of Congress Cataloging in Publication Data

Hildebrand, Grant, 1934–
  Designing for industry

  1. Kahn, Albert, 1869–1942. I. Title.
NA737.K28H54   720'.92'4   72–13358
ISBN 0–262–08054–0

For Judy, Matthew, and Peter

Reyner Banham
Theory and Design in the First
Machine Age

It may well be that what we have hitherto understood as architecture, and what we are beginning to understand of technology are incompatible disciplines. The architect who proposes to run with technology knows now that he will be in fast company, and that, in order to keep up, he may have to emulate the Futurists and discard his whole cultural load, including the garments by which he is recognised as an architect.

CONTENTS

Illustrations   x

Preface   xv

1 INTRODUCTION   1

2 EARLY LIFE AND TRAINING, 1869–1896   5

Childhood in Europe   5

Early Days in Detroit   6

Early Training at Mason and Rice   7

European Scholarship Travel   9

Work as Chief Designer for Mason and Rice   14

Letters and Observations: 1894   16

Constituent Features of Kahn's Background   19

3 KAHN'S PIONEERING INDUSTRIAL WORK, 1896–1916   25

The Young Office   25

Henry Joy and the Detroit Automobile Industry   26

Packard Plant Number Ten   28

The Geo. N. Pierce Plant   34

The Ford Highland Park Plant   43

The Packard Forge Shop   54

Office Structure and Organization   55

Kahn in the Context of His Contemporaries   61

4   EARLY NONINDUSTRIAL VENTURES, 1896–1916   72

Smaller Projects   72

The University of Michigan: Hill Auditorium   72

Second European Trip   80

The Detroit Athletic Club   80

The "Farm," Walnut Lake   87

5   THE FORD ROUGE PLANT AND RELATED PROJECTS, 1916–1932   91

The Impact of the Assembly Line   91

Beginnings of the Ford Rouge Complex: The Eagle Plant   92

Rouge in Expansion: The Glass Plant and Open Hearth Mills   100

The Significance of Rouge   121

Other Industrial Work of the Twenties   124

Office Structure and Organization   126

The Russian Venture   128

6   NONINDUSTRIAL WORK, 1916–1932   133

The General Motors Building   133

The University of Michigan: Clements Library   135

Third and Fourth European Trips   142

The Edsel Ford Home   146

The Fisher Building   147

7 CULMINATION, 1932–1942   152

Economic Recovery   152

Office Structure and Organization   153

The Formulated Approach: The Chevrolet Commercial Body Plant   157

The De Soto Press Shop   165

The Chrysler Half-Ton Truck Plant   172

The Glenn Martin Assembly Building   183

The Glenn Martin Addition, 1939   193

World War II: The Chrysler Tank Arsenal   197

Other Wartime Projects   205

"Beautiful Factories"   206

8 AN APPRAISAL   217

Index   225

ILLUSTRATIONS

Frontispiece: Albert Kahn, Henry Ford, Glenn Martin, and Charles Sorensen

1 European scholarship sketch, untitled, 1891   10

2 European scholarship sketch, Vitré, 1891   11

3 European scholarship sketch, Bruges, 1891   12

4 European scholarship sketch, St. Pierre, Caen, 1891   13

5 Watson M. Freer house, Detroit, 1895, by Mason and Rice   15

6 Plant Number Ten, Packard Motor Car Company, Detroit, 1905   30

7 Geo. N. Pierce Plant, Buffalo, New York, 1906; view of the factory from the northwest   36

8 Geo. N. Pierce Plant; plan and reinforcing bar detail   37

9 Geo. N. Pierce Plant; Manufacturing and Assembly buildings from the roof of the Brazing Building   40

10 Geo. N. Pierce Plant; interior of the Manufacturing Building   41

11 Geo. N. Pierce Plant; interior of the Assembly Building   42

12 Ford Motor Company Plant, Highland Park, Michigan, 1909–; first unit (1909–1910) under construction, from the southeast   46

13 Ford Plant, Highland Park; the first unit in 1909, from the southwest   47

14 Ford Plant, Highland Park; Woodward Avenue elevation   48

15 Ford Plant, Highland Park; typical interior   49

16 Ford Plant, Highland Park; Model T body-to-chassis mock-up   50

17 Packard Motor Car Company Forge Shop, Detroit, 1911; exterior   56

18 Packard Forge Shop; section   57

19 Packard Forge Shop; interior   58

20 Henry B. Joy residence, Detroit, 1908–1909   74

21 Arthur Hill Memorial Auditorium, University of Michigan, Ann Arbor, 1910–1911; exterior   75

22 Hill Auditorium, Ann Arbor; main floor plan and section   76, 77

23 Hill Auditorium, Ann Arbor; interior   78

24 Albert and Ernestine in the Piazza San Marco, Venice, 1912   81

25 The Detroit Athletic Club, Detroit, 1913–1915; exterior   83

26 The Detroit Athletic Club; entrance detail   84

27 The Detroit Athletic Club; lobby   85

28 Summer home of Albert Kahn, Walnut Lake (outside Detroit), 1914–1917   88

29 Ford Motor Company Eagle Plant on the Rouge River, Detroit, 1917   94

30 Ford Eagle Plant; plan   95

31 Ford Eagle Plant; sections   96

32 Ford Eagle Plant; exterior in 1918   97

33 Ford Eagle Plant; interior in 1918   98

34 Ford Glass Plant, 1922; exterior   103

35 Ford Glass Plant; plan   104

36 Ford Glass Plant; section through process lines   105

37 Ford Glass Plant; details of sections   106

38 Ford Glass Plant; details of sections   107

39 Ford Rouge River complex in 1938   110

40 Ford Open Hearth Building, 1925; exterior   113

41 Ford Open Hearth Building; grade-level plan   114

42 Ford Open Hearth Building; mezzanine plan   115

43 Ford Open Hearth Building; sections   116

44 Ford Rouge River complex in 1938, looking north   118

45 Ford Motor Assembly Building, 1924–1925; exterior   119

46 Ford Motor Company Engineering Laboratory, Dearborn, Michigan, 1922; interior   125

47 The General Motors Building, Detroit, 1917–1921; exterior from the northeast   134

48 The General Motors Building; typical floor plans   136, 137

49 The General Motors Building; entrance from West Grand Boulevard   138

50 The General Motors Building; street-level arcade   139

51 The William L. Clements Library, University of Michigan, Ann Arbor, 1920–1921; exterior from the Law Quadrangle   140

52 Angell Hall, University of Michigan, Ann Arbor, 1922–1923; State Street facade   141

53 Rural buildings in Europe, place and date unknown; a photograph from Kahn's trip of 1919   143

54 Europe, place and date unknown; a photograph from the trip of 1919   144

55 Paris, an anonymous building of unknown date; from Kahn's trip of 1921   145

56 St. Ambrogio, Milan, eleventh to twelfth century; atrium; photograph from Kahn's trip of 1921   145

57 The Fisher Building, Detroit, 1927–1929; exterior from the east on West Grand Boulevard   148

58 The Fisher Building; exterior from Second Avenue   148

59 The Fisher Building; main concourse looking south to Second Avenue   149

60 Chevrolet Commercial Body Plant, Indianapolis, 1935; aerial view   159

61 Chevrolet Commercial Body Plant; plan   160

62 Chevrolet Commercial Body Plant; typical sections   161

63 Chevrolet Commercial Body Plant; section through crane bays   162

64 Chevrolet Commercial Body Plant; interior   163

65 De Soto Division Press Shop, Detroit, 1936; exterior of original unit   166

66 De Soto Press Shop; plan   167

67 De Soto Press Shop; sections   168

68 De Soto Press Shop; elevations   169

69 De Soto Press Shop; interior   170

70 De Soto Press Shop; exterior of 1941 addition   171

71 Curtiss-Wright Corporation Stack Shops and Storage Building, Buffalo, New York, 1938   174

72 Curtiss-Wright Storage Building; diagrammatic drawing   175

73 Chrysler Corporation Half-Ton Truck Plant, Detroit, 1937; view along the railroad spur   176

74 Chrysler Half-Ton Truck Plant; plan   177

75 Chrysler Half-Ton Truck Plant; elevations   178

76 Chrysler Half-Ton Truck Plant; sections   179

77 Chrysler Half-Ton Truck Plant; exterior of the Export Building   180

78 Chrysler Half-Ton Truck Plant; interior of the Assembly Building   181

79 Glenn L. Martin Company Plant, Middle River, Maryland, 1929–; rendering of the proposed ultimate scheme   185

80 Glenn Martin Assembly Building, 1937; plan   186

81 Glenn Martin Assembly Building; sections   187

82 Glenn Martin Assembly Building; elevations   188

83 Glenn Martin Plant; exterior of the Assembly Building   189

84 Glenn Martin Plant; exterior of the Assembly Building facing the airfield   190

85 Glenn Martin Plant; airfield facade and interior of the Assembly Building   191

86 Glenn Martin Plant; interior of the Assembly Building   192

87 Glenn Martin Plant; exterior showing the complex in 1939   195

88 Glenn Martin Plant; sections through 1939 addition   196

89 Chrysler Corporation Tank Arsenal, Detroit, 1941; exterior from the northeast   199

90 Chrysler Tank Arsenal; plan   200

91 Chrysler Tank Arsenal; transverse section looking east   201

92 Chrysler Tank Arsenal; interior of final assembly area   202

93 Amertorp Corporation Torpedo Plant, Chicago, 1942   204

94 Curtiss-Wright Corporation Airport Plant, Buffalo, New York, 1941; aerial view   207

95 Curtiss-Wright Plant; exterior of the manufacturing unit   208

96 Curtiss-Wright Plant; exterior of the assembly unit   209

97 Curtiss-Wright Plant; interior of the assembly unit   210

98 Curtiss-Wright Plant; the complex from the airfield   211

99 Albert Kahn at the Farm, Walnut Lake, summer of 1938   212

PREFACE

Albert Kahn maintained an architectural practice in Detroit from 1896 until his death in December of 1942. Though his significant work did not begin to appear until after the turn of the century, his career was of long duration. It was also diverse. His work ranged in size and type from the tiny Clements Library for the University of Michigan to the Willow Run bomber plant of World War II. His contributions, both in industrial architecture per se and in the creation of a new type of architectural practice, are major, as this book intends to show. Nevertheless, there is a dearth of coverage on his career in general and its early industrial contributions in particular. The major published source, George Nelson's *Industrial Architecture of Albert Kahn* (New York: Architectural Book Publishing Co., 1939), is almost exclusively concerned with work from 1934 to 1939, individual examples of which are generally undated and only briefly discussed. Only a few comments are made about Kahn's early life and work, and these have in some cases been modified by more recent scholarship.

Three documentary difficulties exist. First, Kahn was a man of actions, not of words. Maximum use must be made of personal memorabilia and recollections and of the rare occasions when he resorted to speeches or articles. Second, office records, which could supplement these sources with a number of important letters to and from clients, were largely destroyed in 1942. Third, his industrial buildings were not systematically recorded by photographs until the 1930s, a frustrating circumstance when it is realized that unlike most buildings these were especially intended to undergo change. On the positive side, the firm's file of Kahn's working drawings is very complete, and the drawings themselves are superb. I have used them where possible because they have some historical value in their own right and also because they will be appreciated by anyone who enjoys fine draftsmanship. The plan and sections of the Ford Glass Plant, however, have aged too much to reproduce. Mrs. Lois Wardell has graciously redrawn them and has also provided much assistance with typing. Miss Joyce Williams was very kind in giving long hours to the typing of the final draft.

I regard Kahn's industrial work as ultimately more significant than his other designs, and the emphasis in this book reflects that belief. Nonindustrial commissions are grouped in Chapters 4 and 6 for convenience of organization.

All buildings illustrated are extant unless specifically noted as having been demolished. For any who intend to visit extant examples of Kahn's work, however, a word of warning: as noted earlier, the factories were designed to be changed, and most of them have been, some drastically.

For those who are unfamiliar with architectural terms, John S. Scott's *A Dictionary of Building* (Harmondsworth: Penguin Books, 1964) will be helpful.

This book is intended to be an unusual kind of architectural history, and one of its purposes, I hope, will be to direct some attention to large areas of the architectural task that have had very little coverage to date. A satisfaction that comes from tilling relatively little-worked fields is that the soil is not likely to be exhausted. On the other hand, it will be rocky, and the resultant job may be rough. I hope this work leaves fewer rocks and more marked furrows for the next plowman.

Thanks are due to a number of people. Sol King, FAIA, currently President and Director of Architecture of Albert Kahn Associates, Inc., Architects and Engineers, and Mrs. Helen Bunch Deason, Archivist, have always been most helpful. I am also indebted to others of the firm, particularly John Haro and Jay Pettit, for many conversations both during and following my two years' employment there. Kahn's private memorabilia are held principally by his daughters, Mrs. Barnett Malbin and Mrs. Martin Butzel, both of Birmingham, Michigan. They and their brother, Dr. Edgar Kahn, were very warmly helpful. Many who have assisted will, no doubt, disagree on some points of interpretation, however; these points of interpretation are my own.

Professors Hermann Pundt and Thomas Bosworth and Mrs. Ronald Wagner of the University of Washington read drafts of the manuscript, and I appreciate their very valuable suggestions. I could never have undertaken the project at all, for many reasons, without the innumerable occasions of encouragement from Leonard Eaton, mentor and friend; I am happy for this opportunity to acknowledge to him a long-standing debt of gratitude. A portion of this work appeared in the March 1970 issue of the *Journal of the Society of Architectural Historians*; its re-use is by courtesy of the *Journal*.

Finally, my thanks to Judy, my wife. She has earned them many times over.

DESIGNING
FOR INDUSTRY

1
INTRODUCTION

The factory has had varied success in its flirtation with architectural respectability. At the turn of the twentieth century there were very few architects who considered the factory to be worth their notice at all, while the architectural historian, intent on appraising the work of the previous century or so, seemed to be unconscious of the buildings of industry. By 1912 things had changed, especially in Europe. A number of famous architects and also some on their way to fame expressed their enchantment with the technological age, including the factory as one of its symbols, and backed up their enthusiasm by designing factories. From their enthusiasm grew a body of design theory and accompanying movements. World War I brought an additional flurry of interest, as attention turned to the various factory-produced machines of war. But then in the prosperous twenties the factory returned to the fireside while other, more elegant stepsisters went to the ball, in spite of the fact that the twenties saw the growth of the largest and most carefully planned of all industrial complexes, the Ford Rouge River plant outside Detroit. During the depression thirties and the years of World War II the factory gained popular attention again, first as a symbol of employment and then as a symbol of patriotism. It became so ubiquitous that it was impossible to ignore, and it has not since entirely lapsed into its neglected state of former days. Yet bookshelves on architecture still yield meager offerings in the field of industrial building.[1] Some critics, following Wotton's definition of architecture as firmness, commodity, and delight, would no doubt maintain that the industrial building, at least in its usual utilitarian guise and lacking any conscious delightfulness, is not architecture at all. But this argument seems less important than it once did—probably most architectural students today would dismiss it entirely —so that we can, perhaps, include as architecture buildings that have, or have had, a role to play in our man-made physical environment.

Certainly the factory has had its role to play, both because of its significant prevalence and because of the particular kinds of design problems and opportunities that it represents. Let us return, briefly, to the period just before World War I, when the factory as an architectural artifact stood in high esteem indeed. At that time—and in the massive scale to which it had been driven by heavy industry—it was a relatively new building type and one that was rightly felt to be of great importance to the young century. To many it appeared to be an original and significant building type, which offered new challenges. Thus, if its challenges could be answered with equal originality, it held an unusual degree of promise as the potential father of a new and true architectural genre. This was the basis of the symbolic fascination it held for many of the pioneers of the modern movement. Thus, one path of development viewed the factory as the source of a symbolic aesthetic that could be derived at a conscious level and applied to wider levels of experience. This view presumed the architect to be acting in his traditional artistic guise as the conscious interpreter of the spirit of an age, and this was the way taken most notably by Peter Behrens and Walter Gropius. There was another way as well, however, that involved changing one's view of the architect's role, setting aside his traditional aesthetic concerns in order to concentrate almost exclusively on a more complete fulfillment of this building type's practical operational and economic needs. This was an at least equally fertile approach in that it held great promise for real operational solutions, from which new formal patterns could be generated —patterns that had not been part of the original, conscious intent of the designer.

This second approach was the one taken, with great success, by Albert Kahn, who stands as the foremost industrial architect of the early twentieth century. He maintained an architectural practice in Detroit from January of 1896 until his death in December of 1942. During that long career his work was by no means confined to factories. From his office came the General Motors and Fisher buildings for downtown Detroit, many hospitals, residences, social and recreational buildings, newspaper plants, banks, and a large part of the University of Michigan campus at Ann Arbor. But if he had done only these buildings, he probably would be a figure of no more than regional interest. As this introduction has suggested, he emerges as an architect of unique significance because of the design, and the way he set about the design, of well over two thousand factories.

When Kahn founded his practice in 1896, the automobile was being made only as an isolated experiment, almost as a toy, in small backyard garages and shops. As a vehicle for everyday transportation it was nonexistent. The invention of the airplane was seven years in the future. By the end of Kahn's career this picture had changed dramatically; the automobile had been produced in quantities of millions per year, transcontinental and transoceanic aircraft of large capacity were commonplace, and the most mechanized war in history was underway. Thus, Kahn's career coincided with the period in which the heavy mechanized industries of the world grew to maturity. This was fortunate because he was ideally suited to serve this phenomenal growth.

In a way, Kahn was a simple man, with little formal education; theory and the abstract interested him very little. But he had a keen instinct for the urgent practical problem, which interested him very much. His pragmatic approach allowed him to ignore preconceptions to a rare degree in approaching the problems of factory design. He regarded program, structure, and economics as the heart of the problem, and, setting aside formalistic or symbolic purposes, he allowed factual performance criteria to shape the solution. He was also able to see that taking the practical aspects of building design really seriously would in itself be a complex job and would require that performance specialists other than architects per se be a genuine part of the design team, included in decision making from the outset, and not just called in as executors after the key decisions had been made. By putting this realization to use, he created just such a design team. Thus Kahn developed a new view of the role of the architect and his relationship with other areas of expertise; and he demonstrated the importance of this new view by producing an evolutionary series of buildings, demonstrably suitable to their purpose. His approach has led some to consider him an engineer, while still others view his work as vernacular, the product of a completely un-self-conscious design process. But such a view leads us back to Wotton's definition of architecture, which considers it to be not master building in whatever terms one may find it, but rather master building that specifically includes aesthetic purpose. One of the significant aspects of Kahn's career is that he forces us to think again about the usefulness of such distinctions. As an architect he has made large contributions to architecture; but he is especially important because his strengths are not those for which his profession has been noted.

Note

1. For a discussion of the limitations of studies in architectural history over the last decade, see John Maass's "Where Architectural Historians Fear to Tread," *Journal of the Society of Architectural Historians* 28, No. 1 (March 1969): 3–8.

2

EARLY LIFE AND TRAINING, 1869–1896

Childhood in Europe

Albert Kahn was born March 21, 1869, in Rhaunen, a tiny town twenty miles southwest of Mainz, Germany,[1] the first of eight children of Rosalie and Joseph Kahn.[2] Rosalie was a woman of small size but strong character, with an inborn affinity for the visual arts and music. Joseph is remembered as a "highly imaginative and literate person, but not a realist; he lived in a world of fantasy."[3] He was by profession an itinerant rabbi, and so the family traveled often from one town to another until Albert reached school age, at which time they established a home with an aunt in Echternach, Luxembourg. There Albert, as the oldest child, took on some of the responsibility of caring for his many younger brothers and sisters. He also learned to play the piano, and his ability was so exceptional that by the age of seven he was considered a prodigy.

As he grew up in and around Echternach, he found himself situated in one of the most softly pleasant places in Europe, if not in the world. It was, and still is, beautiful country. The hills around are sizable but gentle, covered with forests, and punctuated by trout streams. The foliage is lush. Castles top many of the hills. The valleys are crossed by old masonry viaducts half hidden in the trees. Echternach itself lies in one of these valleys at the juncture of the Sure and the Moselle rivers. Anyone sensitive to visual beauty would remember this region, having once experienced it, and it certainly left rich memories with young Albert. Fifty-odd years later he would recall that "the country around is just the loveliest imaginable. Every square foot carefully planted—mountains—wonderful roads—good-natured, contented villages. It was lovely."[4]

But another aspect of the region might have left an even deeper impression. Seven years before Albert's birth the Krupp family had put into operation at Essen the first Bessemer converter in Germany and one of the first in Europe, marking the beginning of heavy industry in the Ruhr Valley. The Franco-Prussian War of 1870–1871, which resulted in the startling Prussian victory, was won by Krupp guns; they tipped the balance and proved to be by far the most advanced armaments of their time. The plant became famous overnight and throughout the seventies was expanded accordingly. By 1880 Krupp of Essen was literally the arsenal of forty-odd nations. Its technology, especially in large-scale steelwork, established the image that the region still retains a century later. It would be stretching a point to say that young Albert grew up in the shadow of the awakening giant of the Ruhr, but he was only about one hundred miles away as the crow flies, or roughly the distance from London to the Cotswolds; and Krupp's feats were famous and widely publicized. Kahn was even closer to the work of two other Rhinelanders. Throughout the 1870s Karl Benz at Mannheim and Gottlieb Daimler at Cologne were working on the problem of the internal-combustion engine and a motor car powered by it. Each produced a working engine by the end of the 1870s and a working car in 1885. Thus no other region at that time could show more dramatic industrial promise, and no other region could match its strides in the development of the automobile. There is no way of knowing whether Albert heard about or followed any of these developments; we can only conjecture from subsequent events. But it is certainly worth noting that the great industrial era of the Rhineland was in its infancy during his impressionable years, and he was living in close proximity.

Early Days in Detroit

The family stayed in Echternach until 1880, when they emigrated to the United States—to Detroit. Albert's formal schooling was interrupted by the move and was never resumed.

Of his early life in Detroit several things remained in his memory. The first was the stringent life the family was forced to lead. For while the Kahn household may have been well off culturally, economically it was not; the family situation after arrival in Detroit was austere in the extreme. Dreamer that he was, Joseph Kahn was not a remarkably good provider. He tried, and his versatility is amazing: at various times he ran a restaurant, a saloon, and a vegetable garden; tried selling spectacles and sewing machines; and interspersed these activities with engagements as a rabbi in cities as remote as Jacksonville, Florida, and Trenton, New Jersey. But none of these efforts brought an adequate subsistence, and extra income was needed from anyone who could earn it. Because Albert was the oldest of the children, he had to do what he could to shoulder a part of the burden, and he took on all kinds of odd jobs instead of going to school. There can be no doubt that this left an imprint on his entire life. As late as the 1920s, long after he had become a relatively wealthy man, he continued to draw a salary of forty dollars a week, as a symbolic gesture of earlier hard times, and he continued to live modestly. When his own family became a reality, he built an unostentatious house on Mack Avenue in Detroit, which he occupied until the end of his life. There was money for art, music, and travel; for a delightful, though almost modest, summer house on Walnut Lake some twenty miles north of Detroit; and of course for investment, both in his firm and elsewhere; but there was never money for ostentation. Professionally, too, the austerities of youth were of importance. They probably explain his serious approach to problems of economics, and in working out difficulties in a family of ten he would also very quickly have seen the value and the challenge of teamwork. It is also probable that he had to learn to concentrate in order to get things done in what must have been a hectic household, and that, too, would be important to him later.

But in spite of economic difficulties, Rosalie and Joseph Kahn had the wisdom to see longer-range goals and helped Albert toward a job without pay in the architectural firm of John Scott and Company. As he was later to recall: "I had always had a bent for drawing, and despite the fact that at school I got the worst marks in that of anything, my father encouraged me by buying me drawing boards and various materials for sketching. Mother must have thought something of my drawing, for she asked for a job for me in the office of a Detroit architect."[5] The job involved only the most menial work, emptying wastebaskets, running errands, grinding ink, and so on. It lasted, fortunately, less than a year. But it led Albert to accept free drawing lessons with the sculptor Julius Melchers, and that in turn led to a real architectural job, also without pay at first, in the excellent firm of Mason and Rice. Albert began on March 3, 1884.[6] His architectural horizon was brightening.

Early Training at Mason and Rice

In the mid-1880s when Kahn joined the firm, Mason and Rice were designing in the general mode of Henry Hobson Richardson and the shingle style, as were many offices elsewhere in Detroit and throughout the country. What set the firm of Mason and Rice above the norm was not any remarkable individualism in matters of design but rather the great care and sensitivity with which it executed its commissions.[7] Albert Kahn was able to benefit from this quality office, however, largely because of the warmth and interest of the firm's twenty-six-year-old partner George D. Mason.

What a different atmosphere I found here: one of encouragement from the start, for that was Mr. Mason's strong trait. . . .

Work was given to me to do other than mere grinding of ink and running errands. I was taught to draw and make perspectives, to make pen and ink sketches, given a chance at working drawings, at details, and presently my salary was raised to $3.50 per week. . . .

How precious I felt the hours when invited to his house evenings, on East Congress near Dequindre, to help him on the competitive drawings for the Y.M.C.A. which he won, and the Art Museum which he lost, but should have won.

These evenings meant not only experience and practice, but incidentally, a good dinner with a tablecloth and napkins, to none of which I was particularly accustomed at that time.

On these evenings he would often take pains to go through his wonderful collection of photographs with me, and to point out the good and the bad. That proved a large share of what schooling I had.[8]

Thus the opportunity was presented, and Kahn was determined to make the most of it. In spite of the brevity of his formal education, he could draw on a vivid European childhood and a natural sensitivity to the arts, strengthened by his parents' support and by his training with Julius Melchers. Above all he had enthusiastic determination. He was always physically small—an inheritance from his mother—and unathletic, and, as often happens with such men, this may have been a goad to compensatory greater efforts in nonphysical tasks. Mason said of him during these years, "I have never known anyone with such an enormous capacity for concentration and study."[9] Predictably enough, he made rapid progress. By 1888 he was in charge of design and construction of a large residence, the Gilbert W. Lee House, and after that date was given responsibility for most of the residential work in the office.

European Scholarship Travel

Then in 1890, at the age of twenty-one, he was awarded the $500 Travelling Scholarship given by the *American Architect and Building News*. The honor was qualified by the magazine's own admission that the award had the least demanding requirements of any traveling scholarship, and furthermore Kahn was the only applicant that year.[10] But it was an opportunity and he took it. He arrived in Southampton on December 15, 1890, and spent the rest of that year and nearly all of 1891 traveling in England, Belgium, France, Germany, Italy, and, very briefly, Luxembourg. While in Paris he saw the Salon of work from the Ecole des Beaux Arts. He admired the technical skill displayed there but did not like its sense of removal from reality.

> A characteristic feature of the exhibition is the almost total lack of drawings of actually projected work. With us, such drawings form, as a rule, the chief attraction and here they are much missed. The continuous lines of restorations, etc., however excellently drawn, prove almost monotonous to the observer, and even the elaborate school *projets* fail to produce the desired relief.[11]

Toward buildings his tastes were catholic. He visited the usual monuments, and some not so usual. St. Pierre of Caen, for instance, that Renaissance-Gothic amalgam, held a great attraction for him because of its obvious vigor and freedom. The sketches he made of this and other works show how much he had developed his drawing talents. The sketches are beautiful by any standard, showing a keen observation and a sensitive technique (figs. 1–4).

Early in the trip, in February, he met Henry Bacon in Florence. Bacon, later to be architect of the Lincoln Memorial, was a man of much greater wealth than Kahn and of much more extensive formal education—he was traveling on a Roche scholarship of $1,500. But the two men liked each other at once, and Bacon proposed that they travel together for a while. Kahn pointed out that the difference between their budgets suggested they do nothing of the kind, to which Bacon replied that he needed a financial manager, since his money was almost gone. That seems to have settled it. As Kahn said, "we strapped on our packs and walked out of Florence to the next town. . . . Together we traveled and he taught me."[12] As it turned out, they traveled together until late June, when Bacon went to England and Kahn made a pilgrimage to Luxembourg for

Figure 1
European scholarship sketch,
untitled, 1891. (Photograph by
Joseph Klima, courtesy of Mrs.
Barnett Malbin.)

Figure 2
European scholarship sketch, Vitré,
1891. (Photograph by Joseph Klima,
courtesy of Mrs. Barnett Malbin.)

VITRÉ
TOWN WALL.

Bruges August 23rd 1891.

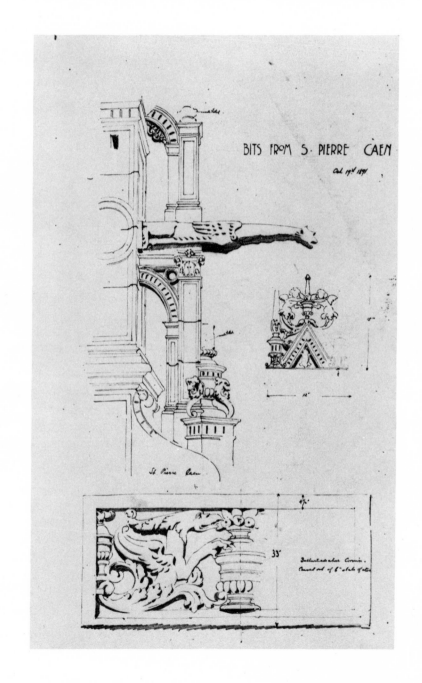

Figure 3
European scholarship sketch, Bruges, 1891. (Photograph by Joseph Klima, courtesy of Mrs. Barnett Malbin.)

Figure 4
European scholarship sketch, St. Pierre, Caen, 1891. (Photograph by Joseph Klima, courtesy of Mrs. Barnett Malbin.)

a six-day stay with relatives. (He listed his Luxembourg expenses in his notes—Bacon had picked a good financial manager—and recorded the side trip in a single sketch of a kitchen rack in an old farmhouse.) The time they spent together was a happy experience for both men, and as a result of it they remained close friends for life.

Kahn often referred to that four months with Bacon as "my real education in architecture," implying that Bacon had served as a knowledgeable, sophisticated guide for the trip. That may have been true to some extent, but it raises an interesting question. Kahn might have visited the usual monuments at Bacon's suggestion, but would Bacon have emphasized the importance of buildings like St. Pierre? That seems unlikely, for while the French Renaissance was certainly enjoying popularity in the 1890s following the precedent of R. M. Hunt's Vanderbilt house, such eccentric buildings as St. Pierre were by no means regarded on an equal plane with, for example, the châteaux of the Loire. The taste for less popular but nevertheless vigorous and dynamic work, toward which so many of Kahn's sketches were oriented, was in all probability Kahn's own. Even at that time he was recording certain attitudes toward architecture that set him apart from his professed guide.

He sailed for the United States late in November of 1891. While abroad he had received frequent "kindly, helpful, instructive letters" from Mr. Mason and noted that "upon my return, with a considerable number of sketches which received rather gratifying comment, no one was happier about the results than Mr. Mason."[13] Apparently that was true enough, because shortly thereafter Kahn was appointed chief designer for the firm.

Work as Chief Designer for Mason and Rice

By his own account the first building he designed in his new position was the Watson M. Freer house, completed in 1895 (fig. 5). By comparison with other Mason and Rice work and with most work of the period, the Freer house appears rigorous, nonpicturesque, and austere. It has little in common with the era of Richardsonian influence then drawing to a close, or with the classicism and eclecticism that were just beginning to gain in popularity. The overall form of the

Figure 5
Watson M. Freer house, Detroit,
1895, by Mason and Rice.
(Photograph by Manning Bros.,
courtesy of W. Hawkins Ferry.)

Freer house is crisp and clear—openings are cleanly incised within the simple mass. The brick has been handled with hardly a trace of romanticism and with great respect for its ability to create a precise wall plane. The house is a personal and original work, sufficiently distinct from previous Mason and Rice designs to have occasioned some office discussion. One can imagine Kahn describing its validity and revealing his sense of the value inherent in an economy of means. This sense served Kahn well in this case; it was fundamental to his later success with industrial commissions.

There is some indication that in 1893 he was offered the position vacated by Frank Lloyd Wright in the office of Adler and Sullivan.[14] This is plausible on two counts: first, some twenty-five years earlier Dankmar Adler had studied under Julius Melchers in Detroit, so there existed a common contact between Adler and Kahn;[15] and second, Louis Sullivan, according to Wright, was looking for "a pencil"[16] in his hand, which to him meant a man of superb drawing ability, and Kahn had demonstrated such ability in his European sketches. In any case, if the offer was made, Kahn declined it. The attributed reason was that he had to help in supporting the family and could not risk giving up his secure position with Mason and Rice, but there could have been another reason, too. In the summer of 1893 Mason and Rice had received a commission to do a residence (now demolished) on Adelaide Street for the Krolik family of Detroit. Kahn was in charge, and he soon developed a personal interest in the daughter Ernestine. The romance must have been underway even in late 1893, because in May 1894, with the knowledge of the two families only, Albert and Ernestine were engaged. Ernestine was a graduate (1892) of the University of Michigan, and the educational difference between her and Albert was of some concern to him from time to time, but apparently that obstacle was not insurmountable.

Letters and Observations: 1894

Late in July of 1894 Ernestine left Detroit for a summer vacation at Sand Beach. She asked Albert not to write frequently since their engagement was unannounced, but he wrote frequently anyway. On August 4, he wrote of the lovely evening and the crowds on Woodward Avenue and of a few hours spent in the Detroit Library. "And what do you think I read in there this evening? I looked up the *Life of H. H. Richardson* by Mrs. Van Rensalaer [sic].[17] You probably know of it. In it there were photos of nearly everything he did—and what masterworks some of them are. . . . How I do wish . . . that I were a Richardson." Two days later he went to Buffalo, partly to find customers for his sister Mollie's new blueprinting business. While there he took the opportunity to see Niagara Falls and loved it. He sought out places not frequented by other tourists and was proud of doing so: " . . . just think I'm the only one here looking, and I know there isn't a spot more beautiful around here, yet the crowds are down below looking at the whole business at once and seeing nothing. . . . Everybody runs where everybody else is." However, he did say that if Ernestine were with him, he would be paying less attention to the scenery. What fascinated him about the falls was the power and scale of the place, which was made more vivid by contrast with areas of intimacy and calm. He wrote glowingly of its immense grandeur and scope, to which he responded even more enthusiastically than he did to the gentler topography of Luxembourg.

You tire of seeing it and yet you can't get away. If those little islands were not right within the cataract it wouldn't be half as beautiful. . . . I just wish you could see me bubble.

I feel just as I did at the world's fair. . . .[18] You see the rocks enclosing the river on all sides apparently, but looking up you have this furious mass of water, on each side and that's not in a straight and hard line but in most graceful curves, bits of land thickly covered with trees, in the center of the picture only water and blue sky with another little spot near the middle. . . .

This roaring current, and right above it the calmest, quietest, bluest sky one would wish to see . . . and then too right in the middle of this wild, impetuous, warring stream, a peaceful, little wooded island, the thick trees on which were hardly moved by a breeze. Always light and shade.

Oddly enough, in terms of his ultimate career, he made no mention of Roebling's magnificent suspension bridge at the Falls, still in existence at the time.

Just as he was about to return to Detroit, he received a telegram from Mr. Mason instructing him to go instead to Larchmont Manor, some eighteen miles outside New York City, to assist Mr. Rice in the on-site development of an estate. He was sorry to be delayed in getting back to

Ernestine, but the trip further broadened his exposure. He spent a few days in New York City with Mr. Rice and was greatly impressed by the just-completed Metropolitan Club by McKim, Mead and White. "Mr. Rice and I stood and stood and couldn't satisfy ourselves. It looks just what it is and I know of few modern buildings that have impressed me so. These men are simply great." And this was not his first contact with their work, for he reminded Ernestine of "their Agricultural Building in Chicago"—the Agricultural Building at the Chicago World's Columbian Exposition of 1893. This admiration for McKim, Mead and White was no fleeting enthusiasm. It remained with him, expressed in his words and his work throughout his life. As late as April of 1931 in an article entitled "Architectural Trend" in the *Journal of the Maryland Academy of Sciences*,[19] he devoted a paragraph to Richardson and "his virile, powerful imagination," then gave five full paragraphs to Charles Follen McKim, "who exerted upon the architecture of our country an influence for benefit which cannot be overestimated." Kahn's letters to Ernestine in 1894 indicate also that he had seen Sullivan's Transportation Building at the Exposition and perhaps some of his work in downtown Chicago as well. It did not excite him as did the work of McKim, though he would recall it, and build on it, in his design for Hill Auditorium in 1911. By 1894, of course, Wright's career had barely begun, and Kahn at that date was understandably unaware of it. When Wright's major works began to emerge later, Kahn acquainted himself with them but was not stirred by them.

Kahn remained with Mason and Rice for just a little more than a year following his trip to the East. Although he had climbed about as high as he could within the office, his ambitions were by no means satiated. He had developed a rapport with two older men in the office, George Nettleton and Alexander B. Trowbridge, both graduates of Cornell and both also holding responsible positions in the office. On January 4, 1896,[20] the three men founded an independent firm under the name of Nettleton, Kahn and Trowbridge.

Thus Kahn's period of training ended, and his professional practice began. Since this practice was to be successful in an unusual way, we should pause to note the unique mental equipment with which Kahn began it.

The first thing to be noted is that he had been admirably successful in building a solid foundation of experience. He had traveled widely. He had seen the great historic buildings of Europe firsthand, and he had been moved by the dramatic topography of this continent. He had worked within the Richardson tradition and become familiar with his life and work through Mrs. Van Rensselaer's biography. Early in his career he had seen the work of McKim, the outstanding conservative architect of his time, and of Sullivan, the outstanding liberal. Clearly, he was an energetic and industrious young man who had sought out and observed a wide variety of experiences. But he had not delineated a position; he had not evolved a particular intellectual or theoretical stance, nor was he the inheritor of one.

This was a matter of both personality and circumstance. When he began with Mason and Rice, lacking any architectural training, he had much to learn about his chosen profession. He was kept busy with the tools and techniques of architecture, in which he had a real interest anyway. A general literary exposure is often conducive to theoretical cogitations, but Kahn had had little time left over to become widely read, a fact about which he himself expressed regret. Though his unliterary adolescence would give him a common bond with some of his clients, most notably Henry Ford, it set him apart from virtually any noted architect of his time.

Frank Lloyd Wright represents the extreme opposite case, and a comparison is illuminating. Wright's *Autobiography*[21] closes with a list of thirty-five titanic minds of history, ranging from Laotze through Goethe, Nietzsche, Melville, and Whitman—these were the men whose thoughts had been assimilated into Wright's mental processes. By contrast, Kahn in his early life could have been familiar with only a few of these men. At Ernestine's urging, he had pored through George Eliot's *Romola,* but it is the only general work of literature he mentions having read in his early years.

The same meager literary grounding taken together with his geographic situation also meant that he was not drawn into either of the two dominant architectural philosophies that might have affected him, namely, the Chicago movement centered on Sullivan and the Ecole des Beaux-Arts based in Paris and also concentrated on the American East Coast.

The movement in Chicago found a literary basis in the writings of Thoreau, Emerson, Whitman, Melville, Ruskin, and perhaps William Morris. It was also marked to a considerable degree by a romantic interest in the ordering principles of nature, particularly as these principles were poetically elucidated in the writings of Sullivan. Furthermore, the movement was primarily composed of Chicagoans. Kahn could not claim an affinity on any of these grounds, and what little he had seen of the movement, in the work of Sullivan and probably others, did not excite him.

As for the Ecole, through three-quarters of a century it had built up a formidable body of academic theory. This theory presumed, first of all, axial planning and, second, an overlay of style derived from historic precedent. So basic were these presumptions that they needed no elucidation or defense. The third and more verbally elaborated aspect of Ecole theory concerned composition, by which was meant the assemblage of masses and the volumes that they created. The influence of this Ecole theory on the East Coast of the United States would be hard to overstate. Certainly it played a major role in shaping more than two generations of architects, from Richard Morris Hunt to the students of Paul Phillipe Cret. But these men were part of a Boston–New York–Philadelphia milieu that did not extend to Detroit. In Europe the Ecole's aura was more or less automatically built into the mental apparatus of just about every major architectural figure, either consciously or subconsciously. It formed the intellectual climate from which Tony Garnier, Auguste Perret, Walter Gropius, and Le Corbusier took their various directions, and though these Europeans made their names by moving from the Ecole's theory in centrifugal fashion, still it was an ineradicable part of their thought processes, always to be found, if only in the wings. With Kahn it was not there either as inspiration or invisible influence. He had visited the Ecole for a day or two during his 1891 trip and was impressed but had reservations.

The only other way in which the Ecole touched him was through stylistic similarities, which he absorbed from the example of his heroes, McKim, Mead and White. These similarities were largely superficial. A great deal of McKim's work was brilliant in terms of Ecole composition, that is, the coherent assemblage of volumes and masses. But this is not what Kahn discusses. He speaks of McKim's artistry, his taste and refinement, his ennobling example, but not of composition in the Ecole sense.

Thus Kahn did not bring to his new practice a deep-running philosophical or theoretical position arising from his own meditations, nor had he absorbed a deeply felt party line. For the usual architectural career this would have been a weakness and perhaps a fatal one, for it would have meant a dependence on derivation, and some of Kahn's ordinary nonindustrial commissions are patently vulnerable to this criticism. But his practice was not to be of the usual sort, and for his particular future he began with an ideally open mental attitude, extraordinarily uncommitted to an expressive, formal, or compositional position. His approach from the beginning was pragmatic, and it continued to be so throughout his career. In a tribute given at the Octagon in 1943, after Kahn's death, Paul Cret could say: "Albert Kahn was not a theorist: the 'architecture of tomorrow' had little interest for one so engrossed in creating the architecture of today."[22]

Kahn also brought to his new practice a number of valuable personal qualities. Mention has been made of his determination, his concentration, and his serious approach to economics. All the evidence also indicates that he had the prized quality of being a good listener. Men of humble beginnings often retain from early life a feeling that the other fellow may know a great deal, that the rest of the world may harbor an unsuspected wealth of knowledge. In some men this feeling is disguised by bluster and a false front; in others it fosters the ability to really listen to what the other fellow has to say, not just out of courtesy but from a belief that his knowledge may be of great value. Whether this is the way it happened with Kahn or not, no one can say, but by all accounts he had this quality to a remarkable degree. It lay behind two of his most important future assets—his ability to form and lead a genuine team and his ability to respond sensitively to his clients' needs. In fact, this ability to listen coupled with a mental attitude free of preconceptions may have been the cornerstone of his unique career.

Finally we must note the influence of the city in which he had matured. Detroit today means automobiles. Anyone who has driven out Woodward Avenue, not to mention Livernois, can sense it in the air (literally, these days). But Detroit did not become an industrial city overnight with the advent of the automobile. In fact, to some extent it was the other way around; the automobile industry lodged there because of the city's industrial history. Bessemer steel had been blown for the first time in the United States at Wyandotte, an outlying town on the Detroit River, in 1864. As a consequence, a bevy of foundries and rolling mills had sprung up, the descendants of which are still there today. Farther east along the river, near the heart of Detroit, Parke, Davis and Company, the pharmaceutical firm, had incorporated and built its factory and offices in 1875. Detroit's D. M. Ferry Seed Company had become the largest in the country. Detroit attracted industry because it was a Great Lakes port and also because it was situated on rail lines from the East through Chicago, and this in turn led it to railroad car manufacture. Rolling stock was being built there as early as 1830. By 1871 the Pullman Company had established a plant there, and from that ti me until well after the turn of the century this was a burgeoning major Detroit industry whose techniques, equipment, and workmen easily made the transition to motorcar making when the time for that came.

As with Kahn's childhood in Echternach, it is hard to say just how much of this activity was known to him. But he can hardly have missed it all, for Detroit then, as now, was unmistakably an industry-based town. Furthermore, in his early odd-job days he had worked in the Michigan Central Depot, where his father had set up a restaurant as one of his many business ventures. Thus Albert would have been in close hourly proximity to the steam locomotives, the basis of Detroit's industry and a potent symbol of the dawning heavy industrial age. These were the engines that some twenty-seven years later were to inspire the Futurists in Milan, who saw the "red-hot bellies of locomotives as they hurtle past at insensate speeds"[23] in terms charged with emotion, poetry, and romance. For Kahn these engines were seen in more practical and workday terms, though their impact may have been as deep, or deeper. The Futurists would express their enchantment with technology by manifestos and visionary projects; Kahn would realize his excitement by designing real factories.

At twenty-six, then, as a principal in his new firm, he was at the brink of his career. With some confidence in his future, he and Ernestine were married on September 14, 1896.

Notes

1. Albert Kahn's daughters, Mrs. Barnett Malbin (formerly Mrs. Harry L. Winston) and Mrs. Martin L. Butzel, both of Birmingham, Michigan, have many of Kahn's personal letters, notes, drawings, European sketches, and so forth, in their possession, as well as, of course, a wealth of personal recollections. Unless otherwise noted, all personal information hereafter may be assumed to be from these sources.

2. Christy Borth, *Masters of Mass Production* (New York: Bobbs-Merrill, 1945), p. 97, implies some doubt about the exact place of birth. The family seems generally agreed on Rhaunen. The children to follow were Gustave, Julius, Mollie, Paula, Moritz, Felix, and Louis.

3. Letter from Mrs. Butzel to the author, July 1967.

4. Letter from Kahn to his daughter Rosalie (Mrs. Butzel), April 3, 1932, from Hotel Scribe, Paris.

5. Quoted in Helen Bennett, "Albert Kahn Gives People What They Want," ms of an article prepared for *American Magazine* and printed, with changes, under the title "You Can't Build Skyscrapers with Your Head in the Sky," Vol. CVIII, No. 6 (December 1929):17ff. The manuscript of the article is in the files of the present Kahn office.

6. The Michigan Society of Architects (MSA), *Weekly Bulletin, Albert Kahn Memorial Issue*, Detroit, May 30, 1943, p. 17, gives the date as January 1, 1885. The 1884 date is from Mr. Mason's own notes.

7. For a detailed examination of Detroit architecture of the time, including that of Mason and Rice, see W. Hawkins Ferry, *The Buildings of Detroit: A History* (Detroit: Wayne State University Press, 1968).

8. From an address given by Kahn on December 7, 1926, at the dedication of the new (second) Masonic Temple by Mason.

9. MSA, *Weekly Bulletin*, May 30, 1943: 17.

10. *American Architect and Building News*, Boston, June 11, 1892, p. 171, and January 3, 1891, p. 1. The *Detroit Free Press* reported that the award was "made without competition because of the knowledge and confidence in the ability of Mr. Kahn, on the part of the publishers of the *American Architect*." That seems unlikely. It would be most unpolitic, and furthermore, the magazine's announcement bemoans the dearth of entries as indicative of apathy.

11. *American Architect* (July 18, 1891): 39.

12. As quoted in the original ms by Bennett, "Albert Kahn," p. 12.

13. Ibid.

14. See George Nelson, *Industrial Architecture of Albert Kahn* (New York: Architectural Book Publishing Company, 1939), p. 283.

15. Hugh Morrison, *Louis Sullivan, Prophet of Modern Architecture* (New York: Museum of Modern Art and W. W. Norton Company, 1935), p. 283.

16. Frank Lloyd Wright, *Autobiography* (New York: Duell, Sloan and Pearce, 1943), p. 68.

17. Marianna Griswold (Mrs. Schuyler) Van Rensselaer, *Henry Hobson Richardson* (Boston: Houghton Mifflin Co., 1888).

18. This was actually a reference to the Chicago World's Columbian Exposition of 1893, some buildings of which he mentions later. The exposition made a lasting impression on him; in an article of April 1931, entitled "Architectural Trend" for the *Journal of the Maryland Academy of Sciences 2*, No. 2: 106–136, he discussed it as though he had just been there: "The composite proved a revelation which left an indelible impress. . . . Who of those who visited this glorious enterprise can ever forget its effect upon him? The exposition seemed a very fairy land. . . . nothing ever done in this country so stimulated our interest in good architecture."

19. Albert Kahn, "Architectural Trend," pp. 113ff.

20. Like Kahn's date of beginning with Mason and Rice, this date has been variously reported. The source for the date used here is, again, Mr. Mason's own notes.

21. Wright, *Autobiography*.

22. Reprinted in *The Octagon, A Journal of the American Institute of Architects* 15, No. 2 (February 1943): 15–16.

23. As quoted in Reyner Banham, *Theory and Design in the First Machine Age* (London: Architectural Press, 1960), p. 100.

3

KAHN'S PIONEERING INDUSTRIAL WORK, 1896–1916

The Young Office

Nettleton, Kahn and Trowbridge practiced under that name for only a short while. In 1897 Trowbridge accepted a position as head of the Department of Architecture at Cornell. The firm then functioned as Nettleton and Kahn through 1900. One of the first commissions was the Children's Hospital on St. Antoine Street. It was a sizable building, simply executed, but it was not a moneymaker. Kahn said of that first year "we made six hundred dollars apiece and if it had not been for the kindness of Mr. Mason in sending us jobs he did not want to tackle it would have been less than that."[1] The Children's Hospital may have been one of the jobs sent over by Mason; the patron of the Hospital was Hiram Walker, an old Mason and Rice client. Perhaps as a result of this commission Nettleton and Kahn designed the Jacobean Grace Hospital Nurse's Home on John R Street in 1898, and in the same year a small library modeled on an English cathedral chapter house was beautifully executed for *Detroit News* founder James E. Scripps.[2] A sketch of a proposed small church was published in the catalog of the First Annual Exhibition of the Detroit Architectural Club of April 1900, and a few residential commissions were mentioned by the *Detroit Free Press,* including remodeling and redecorating for the home of Senator James McMillan. Otherwise, no specific works of the firm from 1896 to 1900, under either name, are known. Apparently other jobs, if any, were small ones, and the firm had not begun to develop in any particular direction. In December of 1900 George Nettleton died, and Kahn was left as the sole principal. The next two years were crucial.

In 1900 he designed his earliest industrial work, a small mill construction factory on Second Avenue in Detroit for Joseph Boyer, manufacturer of pneumatic hammers.

In 1901 he advertised in the *American Architect* for an assistant who might ultimately become a partner. Ernest Wilby responded and in 1902 joined Kahn's staff as chief designer and associate. All work from that date until 1918 went under the title "Albert Kahn, Architect, Ernest Wilby, Associate." Wilby was an Englishman who had graduated from Wesley College, Harrogate, in 1885.[3] Thus he and Kahn were of nearly the same age, Wilby being the elder by only a few years. He seems to have been a capable designer in period styles, and the belief of later members of the firm is that he contributed a facility and distinction that was helpful, perhaps essential, in securing and executing the larger dwellings and small commercial works available to the firm. But it is also worth noting that Harrogate is in the heart of Yorkshire, a county rich in examples of architecture of the early industrial revolution. Wilby would have had an opportunity, at the very least, to familiarize himself with that work.

At the same time, Albert drew his brother Julius into an alliance as chief engineer of the firm. Julius had taken a degree in engineering at the University of Michigan (with financial help from Albert) and had served as a civil engineer for the U.S. military. He and Albert were both interested in the possibilities of reinforced-concrete construction, which they used in their Engineering Building for the University of Michigan at Ann Arbor of 1902–1903 (see chapter 4). Julius thereupon founded the Trussed Concrete Steel Company of Detroit[4] to manufacture his own reinforcing bar design but retained his association with Albert's firm; the two collaborated on concrete building designs well through the next decade.[5]

Here we see for the first time in Kahn's professional life the ability, possibly born of necessity in the large Kahn family, to get along with others in a genuine team fashion. On this occasion one of the team was, of course, his own brother, and though in subsequent years he would draw others of his family into his firm, he could also work exceptionally well with men other than his kin.

Henry Joy and the Detroit Automobile Industry

In 1902 another key event in Kahn's career occurred when Joseph Boyer, Kahn's first industrial client, introduced him to Henry B. Joy. Joy was the son of James Joy, organizing force for several railroad, bridge, and canal companies, president of the Michigan Central Railroad, director of the Detroit National Bank, and at one time regent of the University of Michigan. Henry Joy was thus immersed in the social, financial, industrial, and educational affairs of southeastern Michigan. He was a member of the Detroit Golf and Country Club and later a founder and president of the Detroit Athletic Club, from both of which Kahn subsequently received large commissions. Joy probably supported the selection of Kahn as architect for the Engineering

Building at Ann Arbor of 1902–1903 and almost certainly for the Helen Newberry Women's Residence of 1914–1915, named for Joy's wife.[6] Most importantly, in 1903, Henry Joy became manager of Packard Motor Car Company and appointed Kahn as architect for the firm. Thus, from Henry Joy came many of Kahn's nonindustrial commissions and also his first work for the Detroit automobile industry.

Detroit's relationship with the automobile goes back to at least 1896 when Charles King and Henry Ford drove motorcars of their own construction on the streets of Detroit. Both cars were one-of-a-kind projects, however, and so were not the determining factor in Detroit's involvement with automobile manufacture. But in Lansing, Ransom E. Olds built a car earlier than either Ford or King, which he sold in 1893 in New York City.[7] This is the first record of the automobile as a commercial article, implying production as well as invention. In 1899 Olds founded the Olds Motor Works in Detroit. In 1901, 425 curved-dash Oldsmobiles were built, followed by another 2,500 in 1902. That was by far the largest volume manufacture of automobiles at the time, and it marked Detroit as the center of automotive industry.

It was Olds' success that fixed the center of the automobile industry in that city. It is equally true that the Olds Motor Works was the first to reach quantity production by applying the progressive system of assembly to the manufacturing of a single model gasoline-engine-driven vehicle, and the first to popularize the automobile with the American people, taking it from the classification of a rich man's toy to that of every man's servant.[8]

This was not Olds's only contribution. "More people were either trained or introduced to the potential of the automobile in those early days by him than by any other individual."[9] Those involved with early Olds production included Fred J. Fisher, the Briscoe brothers, John and Horace Dodge, Henry M. Leland, Roy Chapin, and John Maxwell. From 1902 to 1905 Olds was shifting his production center from Detroit to Lansing, but the automobile-minded men just mentioned remained in Detroit, and to their ranks were added such figures as Henry Joy and Henry Ford. Ford's founding of the Ford Motor Company in 1903 was the event that in retrospect seems to have put the final stamp on Detroit's claim as the center of the automobile industry.

Henry Joy had been a good friend of Charles King in the 1890s and had also been involved in the production of marine engines, so he was interested in the automobile probably well before the turn of the century. From his father's concerns he had become familiar with the worlds of industry and finance. In 1901 he persuaded James Ward Packard, then building automobiles at the New York and Ohio Company in Warren, Ohio, to establish a plant in Detroit. By 1903 this had become the main plant for the renamed Packard Motor Car Company, and Joy was its manager.

It was at that point that he secured Albert Kahn as company architect. Joy knew other architects, no doubt, yet he chose Kahn, not for a single building, but for all of the company's projects. As Kahn himself suggested, it may have been that no other architect was interested in this kind of work. But for a man of Joy's sophistication, interest alone would not have been quite enough—he would have had to sense ability as well. Apparently even in 1903 Kahn was able to talk about industrial problems and solutions with an insight and conviction that distinguished him from his colleagues. And probably his enthusiasm was transparent—Rosalie, his youngest daughter, sensed that "the excitement of the growing industry possessed him."

Packard Plant Number Ten

Kahn's early designs for Packard were conservative; from 1903 to 1905, nine factory buildings were done in conventional mill construction. Of these, the first seven, all designed by May 30, 1903, comprised the heart of the plant. They were organized in a quadrangle with Buildings Five and Six at the center of the courtyard. The complex included a machine shop, power building, stockroom, assembling room, offices, and so on, but no particular order of arrangement is discernible.

Then in 1905 Albert and Julius Kahn designed Packard Plant Building Number Ten of reinforced concrete (fig. 6).[10] The site was the Packard grounds, where the first nine units had been erected, on the north side of Grand Boulevard between Packard Avenue and Concord

Avenue, served by a Michigan Central spur along Packard. Building Ten was originally modest in size, a two-story structure measuring in all 60 feet north to south by 322 feet east to west.[11] Columns were located at intervals of 32 feet 3 inches along the centerline of the building, supporting a girder on which beams rested at 16-foot 1/2-inch intervals. The opposite ends of these beams were supported directly on columns spaced at 16-foot 1 1/2-inch intervals along the outside wall. Thus no girder was necessary at the outside wall, so that glass could extend up to the ceiling, where it was of greatest importance in lighting the interior. The 32-foot 3-inch interior spacing was somewhat greater than the usual mill construction spans, and it gave an impressive roominess to the interior. Otherwise, the planning is not particularly innovative and is in fact similar to that of the earlier Packard work. (The two upper floors shown in figure 6 were added before 1909. The drawings indicate that they were anticipated from the beginning, and column sizes and details were developed accordingly.) On the exterior the structural frame was simply exposed. The lower part of the bay, in which glass would provide little increase in illumination, was filled with a brick panel that carried a concrete sill. Asymmetry and irregularity in bays and members were accepted where necessary to follow functional and structural needs.

The Trussed Concrete Steel Company under Julius Kahn's direction was responsible for the structural engineering and detailing. The basic reinforcing element was a continuous bar to resist tension along the bottom of the beam or girder with frequent projections upward and outward toward the ends to counter diagonal tension stresses. To achieve this configuration a bar of square cross section was used, placed on edge, with continuous wings to either side, which could be bent upward at 45 degrees as needed. The device was patented as the "Kahn System of Reinforced Concrete." (The Kahn bar in one of its versions is illustrated in figure 8.)

The advances of Plant Number Ten over the previous nine Packard buildings by the Kahns are easy to enumerate: it reduced significantly the frequency of interior columns (maximum bay size in the earlier buildings was 16 feet by 25 feet); it was fireproof; its walls were opened to a degree far greater than the earlier nine plants, which had the usual arched windows that did not

go fully to the ceiling and were laterally separated from one another by three feet of brick wall. Thus Plant Number Ten represented a clear advance in factory construction for Packard and for the automobile industry in general, as it was the first automobile plant to be built of reinforced concrete. But since it marked Kahn's serious entry into the broader field of industrial architecture, it must be measured against the general context of developments in that field, for which a brief historical review is in order.

The early factories of the industrial revolution in England were typically multistory, bearing wall structures with heavy floor and roof construction. Windows were usually of modest size. Such buildings continued to be built well into the twentieth century (as already mentioned, Kahn's first nine buildings for Packard were of this type). But cast iron was used as early as 1797 for the columns and beams of the five-story Benyon, Marshall and Bage Flax Mill at Shrewsbury, England; and by the middle of the nineteenth century there was considerable experimentation in the use of iron framing, notably in the imaginative work of James Bogardus of New York. The years from 1840 to 1860 also saw a number of patents issued for basic truss designs. Examples of these executed in iron were in use to a limited extent by the end of the century, in some cases with an imaginative integration of clerestory lighting. Elaborate forms of the iron roof with provision for light admission were, of course, a common feature of the great Victorian train sheds in both the United States and Europe. Though these cannot precisely be termed industrial buildings, they were unquestionably a catalyst for the development of industrial iron framing, as were the well-known Chicago skyscrapers of Jenney, Burnham, Sullivan, and others. The pioneer in the steel-framed factory was Charles Caldwell, who in 1904 designed an exposed steel-framed structure for the Fischer Marble Company at 290 Locust Avenue in the Bronx. This two-story building employed tubular steel columns made of two channels welded together, supporting steel girders, wood joists, and a wood floor. Windows ran from a low brick sill wall to the steel spandrel beam above.[12]

Exposed iron and steel as factory structural materials have three disadvantages: they are not

Figure 6
Plant Number Ten, Packard Motor Car Company, Detroit, 1905. (Photograph by J. McCaushey, courtesy of Albert Kahn Associates.)

fireproof, their relatively low deadweight provides little vibration damping when used for superimposed floors, and maintenance painting is required in the corrosive industrial atmosphere. Such problems are more serious in multistory than in single-story buildings but are largely obviated by the use of reinforced concrete. Its history as a technique dates from 1848 when the Frenchman Joseph Lambot built a rowboat of concrete reinforced with iron rods. Seven years later his countryman François Coignet secured a patent for two-way reinforcing in floors, and in 1867 Josef Monier, also a Frenchman, secured a patent for reinforcing in columns and beams, though it is doubtful that these men understood very well the principles at work. (They seem to have regarded the reinforcing as generally knitting the concrete together, rather than as a discrete tensile element of a composite system.) The first complete architectural work in reinforced concrete in the United States was the William E. Ward house in Port Chester, New York, of 1876, for which Ward himself was the structural designer.

In 1877 Thaddeus Hyatt, a New York inventor, worked in London with David Kirkaldy, pioneer in the field of industrial testing machines. Together they conducted a series of experiments in the behavior of reinforced concrete, from which dates the beginning of a scientific understanding of the proper forms of reinforcing to resist tension in beams, slabs, and columns. Hyatt also made the essential discovery that thermal expansion and elongation under stress are virtually the same for both the concrete and the reinforcing element. Starting in 1879 three Germans, E. A. Wayss, Rudolph Schuster, and K. Koenen, advanced markedly the scientific knowledge pertaining to construction of a wide variety of structures. In 1892 François Hennebique was given a patent for the most scientifically advanced system to that date, which included such features as stirrup reinforcing[13] against shearing stress (whose existence and nature he had defined in 1880), reinforcing in the tops of members subjected to negative moments because of continuity,[14] and bending up of the tension bars at their ends to assist in countering diagonal shear.

In the United States, with the exception of the Ward house already mentioned, the major efforts before 1900 were those of Ernest Ransome. From 1888 to 1898 he designed and had a number of buildings constructed in California in which his system of reinforcing by twisted bars of square cross section underwent continuous evolution. In 1898 his firm was both designer and contractor for the Bayonne, New Jersey, plant of the Pacific Coast Borax Company, which exemplifies the development of Ransome's system at the time. The structure consisted of solid concrete columns supporting a frame of girders, beams, and closely spaced joists all poured integrally with the floor slab. Four stories were built thus, reinforced throughout with Ransome's usual twisted square bars. Single bars were placed at the tops and bottoms of beams and joists, probably as a result of Ransome's knowledge of Hennebique's work.[15]

Ransome's practice continued through the turn of the century. His most impressive work was the remarkable plant for the United Shoe Machinery Company in Beverly, Massachusetts, in 1903–1905. This immense four-story structure provided sixteen acres of floor area and utilized a clean, largely unornamented, precisely articulated concrete frame whose voids were filled by a curtain wall of glass.[16]

If we compare Albert Kahn's Packard Plant Number Ten with the slightly earlier work of Ransome and Caldwell, we must conclude that it represented only a limited advance over those buildings. Its complete lack of ornamentation could be seen as forward-looking by comparison with Ransome's work, though Caldwell's plant is equally spare. The 32-foot spans of Packard are noteworthy for a multistory industrial building, but other buildings of different types had exceeded this span in concrete. The proportion of exterior wall given over to windows was slightly greater than that of Caldwell's plant and slightly less than Ransome's. The Kahn bar reinforcing system had a certain attractive theoretical efficiency in that its shear reinforcing wings, bent upward at 45 degrees, acted approximately parallel to the forces tending to cause fracture;[17] but the Kahn bar was unquestionably difficult to fabricate, and it did not easily permit hooking of the ends of members to develop bond stress.[18] Furthermore, the use of the projecting wing as shear reinforcement imposed a limitation on either the length or the spacing of the shear reinforcing elements; that is, the closer the spacing, the shorter the member, and vice versa. In these respects the Ransome system had the advantage; consequently it, and not the Kahn bar, was the prototype of future methods.

But if we must qualify the intrinsic importance of the Packard Building, nevertheless in other ways it played a significant role: in the race that the development of industrial architecture represented, it marked the passing of the baton to Kahn, and it shifted the race to the fast track of the automotive industry. It also indicated Kahn's readiness to try what was an unusual path for an architect—putting aside the formalistic paraphernalia of the typical practice to try a less glamorous kind of design determined solely on practical grounds. This was not, and still is not, the way to conventional professional prestige. There was a fee to be realized, admittedly. Still, his approach commands admiration. He must have felt confident and at home in this work, and excited by it, in order to have been lured away from the more obvious temptations of the usual architectural image.

The Geo. N. Pierce Plant

The Packard plant was quickly followed by another factory whose intrinsic importance is not shared by any other building of its time and can hardly be overstated. It is a prototype factory whose planning principles laid the foundations of factory design for the next several decades. This is the little-known Geo. N. Pierce Plant of Buffalo, New York, built in 1906 for the manufacture of the Pierce Great Arrow (later Pierce Arrow) car. The design was a collaborative effort involving Albert Kahn, the Trussed Concrete Steel Company, and Lockwood, Greene and Company, an architectural firm of Boston.

On the completion of the plant a 24-page booklet was issued by the Trussed Concrete Steel Company to describe the plant in detail, illustrated with eighteen photographs and a plan.[19] According to this booklet the three firms began the design in April 1906. The buildings were essentially completed and turned over to the owners by the first of November, "although the work of installing the heating system, plumbing, etc., took some two months longer."[20] The Trussed Concrete Steel Company was responsible for structural engineering and for supervision of construction. The exact contributions of each of the two architectural firms were not specifically stated and are more difficult to determine. Lockwood, Greene and Company did an appreciable amount of factory work subsequent to the Pierce Plant, though most of their plants are multistory schemes for nonautomotive industries.[21] As for Albert Kahn's retention by Pierce, we must assume that this came about because of his Packard work; and although three years' experience may not seem decisive now, at that time it encompassed virtually the whole history of automobile factory design in this country.

The site was a 15-acre tract at the northeast corner of the Pan American Exposition Grounds, bounded by Elmwood Avenue on the west and the New York Central Belt Line on the north. On this site were disposed the eight separate buildings of the complex (see figs. 7 and 8).

The Administration Building fronted on Elmwood Avenue. It measured 67 feet by 250 feet and consisted of a basement and two upper floors, the topmost of which was roofed by semicircular arches spanning the 67-foot distance.[22]

The Garage, the Brazing Building, and the Power House formed a group ranged along the north edge of the site, where they could be directly serviced by the railroad spur. The Garage was a one-story building 55 feet by 139 feet lighted by wall windows and by a central monitor[23] running continuously across all interior bays, the roof being held up by "unsupported [sic] beams of reinforced concrete . . . 55 feet in length [to provide] unobstructed floor area."[24] The beams were 16 inches by 56 inches at the center of the span, tapering to a shallower depth at each end, with a maximum of 12 square inches of reinforcing steel. The Brazing Building was very similar but 377 feet long and with a row of columns at 25-foot intervals along its centerline.[25] Because of the high temperatures in the Brazing Building, all monitor glazing could be opened by pivoting the sash and was operable "from the floor by a special device"[26] to provide ventilation. The western portion of the Power House was identical to the Garage except in length. The remainder of the Power House was a series of spaces of varying heights and lesser spans.

Figure 7
Geo. N. Pierce Company "New
Automobile Plant," Buffalo, New
York, 1906; view of the factory from
the northwest showing all buildings
of the complex. The Garage, Brazing
Building, and Power House are in
the foreground; the low sawtooth
roof immediately beyond covers the
Manufacturing Building; and the
high sawtooth roof is the Assembly
Building. (Photograph by Joseph
Klima, courtesy of Mrs. Barnett
Malbin.)

Figure 8
Geo. N. Pierce Plant; plan and reinforcing bar detail. Note the interrelated structural modules of the Manufacturing, Assembly, and Body buildings and the broad expanse of the Manufacturing-Assembly unit, made possible by roof lighting. The alternating bar is an improvement over the earlier Packard type whose diagonal members did not alternate. (Photograph by Joseph Klima, courtesy of Mrs. Barnett Malbin.)

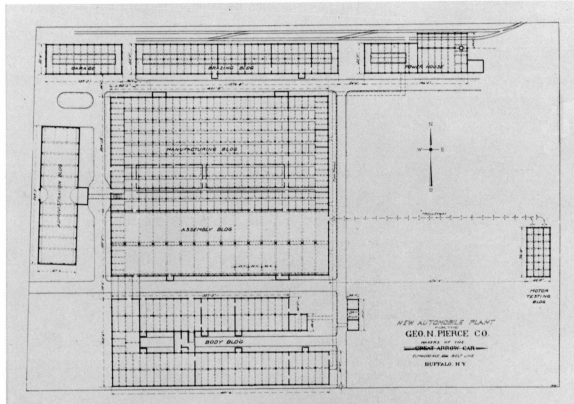

Block Plan of "The Typical Factory."

Kahn Trussed Bar, Alternating Type

The Motor Testing Building, essentially very similar to the Brazing Building, was at the east edge of the site.

The remaining three buildings—the Manufacturing, Assembly, and Body buildings (fig. 9) —were the heart of the plant. They were interrelated programmatically and structurally. The Manufacturing Building was a one-story structure 205 feet by 401 feet, with 25-foot by 20-foot 6-inch structural bays; a sawtooth roof supported on concrete bents provided natural light regularly across the entire floor area. The window sash in the sawtooth roof was made stationary, "having plank frames and double glazed windows. . . . A row of Globe ventilators in each bay, 50 feet apart, provides for ventilation."[27] The interior of this building is shown in figure 10; the 8-inch I beams running from girder to girder were used only to support the drive shafting and machinery and were not part of the primary structural system.

The Assembly Building (fig. 11) was also of one story but much higher than the Manufacturing Building with which it was contiguous. It utilized the same east-west column spacing, but beams 16 inches wide and 93 inches deep, which were reinforced with 18 square inches of steel, spanned 61 feet in the north-south direction and created a building with two vast column-free interior spaces, each 61 feet wide and 401 feet long.[28] A three-ton crane, supported on concrete girders, traveled the length of each bay. Again a sawtooth roof was used, but it ran perpendicular to that on the Manufacturing Building. The Body Building, lying to the south across a 40-foot alley, was a two-story structure in which each floor was half the height of the Assembly Building, so that the two buildings shared a common eave line. The Body Building consisted of two wings each 60 feet wide; the structure of each consisted of two 30-foot spans. The second floor of the Body Building was connected to the upper part of the Assembly Building by a bridge 50 feet wide, which crossed the 40-foot alley in a single span.

The primary structure in all buildings of the Pierce Plant was of reinforced concrete. Structural design techniques, with the exception of the Administration Building, did not differ radically from those used in the Packard Plant, the differences being reflected in two areas: refinements of detail, such as the alternating upturns of the reinforcing bar; and a greater versatility of usage, for example, the sawtooth bents.

Yet in almost every other respect the Pierce Plant was of the greatest significance. The various operations were located in buildings of varying structural requirements, but all were related along lines of circulation determined by the flow of the work. Raw material arrived by train or truck and was transmitted directly to the receiving room located in the Brazing Building. From there it proceeded to the east or west faces of the Manufacturing and Body buildings to be processed along an east-west flow. The work then moved laterally to the Assembly Building to enter the assembly process at the appropriate point. The completed car emerged from the west side of the Assembly Building for transfer to the Garage, from which it could embark directly by rail or truck. The three main buildings were interrelated by a common structural module, which, through permutations of multiples and submultiples, determined the locations and lengths of the various supporting members. Because most of the plant was organized on a single floor, the manufacturing process itself became horizontally organized, and the roof could be used to light all areas. Thus roof lights could and did supply natural illumination for virtually the entire plant. Once roof lighting had become possible for most operations, the plan dimensions were no longer limited by considerations of light penetration from wall windows. Blocks of floor space could then increase in width and length without limit as the industrial process might dictate, and related functions could be located contiguously. The plan, and the manufacturing process itself, assumed a broad, rectilinear configuration suggesting mechanized horizontal circulation against which the wide column spacings, as in the case of the Assembly Building, would provide a minimum of friction. Thus the Pierce Plant introduced into automobile factory design the one-story, roof-lighted, wide-span format of unlimited horizontal dimensions, and as such its importance can hardly be overemphasized. This plant seems so ideally suited to assembly-line operations that it

Figure 9
Geo. N. Pierce Plant; Manufacturing and Assembly buildings from the roof of the Brazing Building. The Body Building is at the extreme right. (Photograph by Joseph Klima, courtesy of Mrs. Barnett Malbin.)

Figure 10
Geo. N. Pierce Plant; interior of the Manufacturing Building showing the concrete structure and the I beams to support shafting. (Photograph by Joseph Klima, courtesy of Mrs. Barnett Malbin.)

is startling to realize that they were not used there when the plant was completed and in fact were not used in automobile production until 1913, nearly seven years after the Pierce design.

The speed with which this plant was erected also deserves mention, since timing was and would continue to be a crucial concern within the industry. The Pierce Company was well aware of the importance of getting a plant in operation as soon as possible and had selected the architects and the design on the basis of potential early completion of the work. From that standpoint, too, the new plant was a success. The time from beginning the design to actual occupancy was at most a matter of nine months, and "the structural work on the plant, covering an area of over 280,000 square feet, was completed in approximately six months time, or exactly one-half the time required by contractors using the ordinary methods."[29]

The Ford Highland Park Plant

The Packard and Pierce work led to the selection of Kahn by the greatest single auto maker of all, Henry Ford. Their first contact came no later than mid-1908. The *Detroit News Tribune* of September 20 reported a Ford plant by Kahn as an example of reinforced-concrete construction; the building, though not exactly identified in the newspaper, must have been the new Highland Park Plant, then in early design stages. Ford had announced the Model T in March of 1908, and his mind had already turned to the consideration of a new and better factory for producing it. He had confidence in his new car and was sure that the existing Piquette Plant would be inadequate to produce the volume he felt would be demanded.

No doubt, Ford was led to the choice of Kahn through the reputation of Kahn's factory work, and particularly the Packard Plant, which was only a few miles from the site Ford had in mind. But the personalities of the two men were also similar. Like Kahn's, Ford's interests lay in down-to-earth innovation; his love was for the applicable, tangible aspects of a problem. A natural mechanic, he evolved his skills and talents pragmatically. In his later years, Ford was mercurial, cantankerous, and obstinate, without any doubt; but he was also enthusiastic, energetic, and determined; and the latter qualities he certainly shared with Kahn. When the two men discussed a problem, they must have talked a similar language. Kahn said he was the listener in their conversations, but innumerable sources make it clear that Ford had no use for those who only listened. He wanted a man to offer ideas or, even better, work hard to amplify and carry through the directions he had in mind, and Kahn more than any other architect available seems to have been the man for that. Furthermore, Kahn's meager formal education, which up to now had appeared to be a handicap, was in this instance a real advantage. Ford lacked extensive schooling himself and tended to scorn it in others; in Kahn he had a man with just the expertise required but with no pretenses to that erudition which so irritated him. It is not surprising that theirs was a long relationship. Even during the twenties, when Ford's *Dearborn Independent* was publishing its anti-Semitic series of articles, Ford and Kahn seem to have been held together by common bonds.[30] Ultimately Kahn would do more factories for Ford than for any other manufacturer, and Ford work would be the cornerstone of Kahn's practice in the prosperous twenties.

The site that Ford had in mind for the new Model T factory was a 230-acre plot on Woodward Avenue in Highland Park, which at that time was several miles outside the periphery of greater Detroit. The site was served by the Detroit Terminal Railway, a belt line connected to every railway entering Detroit. The new plant was in design development in the latter part of 1908 and early 1909 and was first occupied on New Year's Day of 1910.

The original unit was a four-story building 860 feet in length and 75 feet in depth, fronting on Woodward Avenue at the corner of Manchester Avenue. Columns were spaced at 20-foot intervals along the 860-foot length; three 25-foot bays made up the 75-foot depth. Continuous girders spanned these 25-foot bays and carried the 20-foot beams spaced at 8-foot 4-inch intervals. The slab was poured integrally with the beams. Four utility elements, including elevators, stairs, and toilet rooms, abutted the east facade. These were located outside the main body of the building in order to leave the open loft space of the manufacturing unit uninterrupted. Thus, in its basic format the Ford Highland Park building was similar to Packard Plant Number Ten but with somewhat reduced spans (figs. 12, 13, 15). On the exterior the corners and cornice received a kind of vestigial ornamentation in contrast to the starkness of Packard, but the structural grid itself was treated with great clarity and precision. The outer surfaces of vertical and horizontal members were held to the same plane, reflecting the essential continuity of the frame. The sash was of steel, imported from England. It was of maximal size and was uninterrupted by any major mullion subdivisions, so that it gave the impression of being a taut skin or screen, quite different from that given by the double-hung sash at Packard and Pierce (fig. 14).

Ford has often been quoted as saying that for Highland Park he wanted a building that would consolidate all operations under one roof and all major operations on one floor. Since this would suggest a solution similar to Pierce, we must know something about the unique aspects of the manufacturing methods at both the Piquette Plant and Highland Park (in its first few years) to understand what was needed and why the building was designed as it was. At the earlier Piquette Plant Ford had begun to use gravity chutes to transfer some parts and materials from one operation to another, though not on a systematic or widespread basis. But late in 1908 he had predicted that Piquette production figures would be multiplied by five in the new plant, and to do that he was counting on a highly systematized and organized work process with maximum utilization of gravity for transport of raw materials, parts, and subassemblies—hence the necessity for a multistory scheme. Raw materials were to be hoisted to upper levels to filter down by gravity chutes through the various processes of manufacturing, and subassemblies, including units as large as the entire body with seats and doors installed, were to be transferred by these chutes. Thus the building was conceived as a three-dimensional matrix or grid whose planning relationships had to be studied not only within each floor but also from one floor to another. The exterior view (fig. 16), though of a late addition, illustrates a mock-up of one of the last phases of operations in which the body drops onto the chassis; this operation was actually performed in the interior of the plant.[31] Interesting as it was, this approach to the housing of manufacturing was soon to be outmoded with Ford's introduction in this same plant of the powered moving

Figure 12
Ford Motor Company Plant,
Highland Park, Michigan, 1909–;
the first unit (1909–1910) under
construction, from the southeast.
(This plant was demolished ca. 1960.
Photograph courtesy of Ford
Archives, Henry Ford Museum.)

Figure 13
Ford Plant, Highland Park; the first
unit in 1909, from the southwest.
(Photograph courtesy of Ford
Archives, Henry Ford Museum.)

Figure 14
Ford Plant, Highland Park;
Woodward Avenue elevation. The
first unit of the complex-to-be, with
the Administration Building to the
front. The concrete frame is handled
with great precision and is
completely infilled with English steel
sash. (Photograph courtesy of Albert
Kahn Associates.)

Figure 15
Ford Plant, Highland Park; typical
interior. (Photograph courtesy of
Albert Kahn Associates.)

Figure 16
Ford Plant, Highland Park; Model
T body-to-chassis mock-up. In one-
story schemes this operation was
performed in the usually high-
ceilinged assembly room.
(Photograph courtesy of Albert Kahn
Associates.)

assembly line. Within five years of the opening of Highland Park, Henry Ford would turn his thoughts to a new manufacturing complex, and within seven years the company would embark on a policy of one-story buildings to the virtual exclusion of the multistory scheme.

This development leads us to a further evaluation of the Highland Park plant in the context of some pertinent remarks by Kahn:

> When Henry Ford took me to the old race course where the Highland Park plant stands and told me what he wanted, I thought he was crazy. No buildings such as he talked of had been known to me. But I designed them according to his ideas. Ford's big contribution to industrial building is the covering of many activities with one roof and thus saving expense in building, heating and upkeep.[32]

This appraisal needs a bit of scrutiny because it is misleading on some points. First, the idea of a number of activities under one roof did not originate with Ford. The earliest textile mills of the industrial revolution grouped all activities under one roof, to name one obvious example. In terms of the automobile industry, Kahn's own Pierce Plant also provides a prior example in which small parts manufacture, body work, and assembly took place under one roof. Thus the attribution of this idea to Ford is not strictly correct, though it would be correct to say that Highland Park exploits the idea effectively. Second, Kahn's comment further implies that this all-under-one-roof feature was of significance to later work. But later on, when Ford began again at a different site, he did not combine activities under one roof as at Highland Park but instead provided almost total autonomy among activities. Thus the Highland Park Plant is an interesting example in the evolution of an architecture for industrial production, but it is not quite as original as Kahn perhaps believed it to be, nor is it a prototype of the most significant future work.

America's love-at-first-sight response to the Model T needs no elaboration here; production of the Model T was roughly doubling each year from 1908 through 1913, and as a consequence the Highland Park Plant was in a continuous state of growth. The Administration Building and the Power Plant, both located between the Main Building and Woodward Avenue, were underway in 1910. From the south end of the Main Building a similar unit was run northward along John R Street. A one-story machine shop completely filled the U formed by these buildings. The machine shop was steel-framed with a sawtooth roof and with 57-foot craneways bisecting it both from north to south and from east to west. In 1914–1915 a six-story unit was built across John R Street to the east along Manchester Avenue. This unit was similar to the original in appearance but was of flat slab construction with two steel-framed, skylighted craneways of full height. An interesting feature of this unit was that hollow concrete columns carried ductwork for air distribution.

This later work was not entirely by Kahn; Edward Gray, construction engineer for Ford, appears to have designed a great many of the additions.[33] But since they enlarged upon the theme of the original unit by Kahn, a summation of their qualities is pertinent here.

The buildings were unique and different from previous factory construction. They had a craneway between each pair of buildings, the roof of the craneway being glass, so that there was a continuous light well the length of the building. It was not necessary to put sides in those buildings, other than the street side, so that the buildings were not encumbered with walls or partial walls. The heating plants with air washers were on the roof so that they could not only heat, but also ventilate and cool the buildings. The waste air on its way out of the building heated the craneway without any expense.

Galleries were built on either side of the craneway, to enable workmen to unload a car of material or a car of finished product directly from any point in the gallery. The design of the building was such that raw material was hoisted as near the roof as possible, letting it work down in the process of manufacture. Thousands of holes were cut through the floors so that the parts that started in the rough on the top floor gravitated down, through chutes, conveyors, or tubes, and finally became a finished article on the ground floor.[34]

The preceding comments deal with technical considerations exclusively, but they suggest an important point with regard to the design of Highland Park in particular and factories in general. To most manufacturers good design was seen in terms of improved production; with better work conditions quotas could be increased. Henry Ford said quite candidly of Highland Park, "You know, when you have lots of light, you can put the machines closer together"—in other words, less wasted space and time between operations and more production processes per square foot of plant constructed.[35] This is corroborated by pictures of workmen at very closely spaced stations at Highland Park. The Ford Educational Department in 1916 reflected a similar point of view; it declared that from a business standpoint the brighter factory environment was one of "the very best investments"[36] the Ford Company ever made. On the other hand, we tend to see improved working conditions as related to humanistic rather than technical ends, and particularly to the comfort and well-being of the worker. There is every reason to think that both Ford and Kahn considered and valued these ends as well. This was a period of high idealism in humanitarian concerns at Highland Park. The whole issue of worker welfare was being considered in terms ranging from home life anxieties to appeal methods for discharge, and Ford was also setting an example in the hiring of the physically handicapped and former convicts. But the preceding quotations suggest that production concerns rather than humanitarian ones were primary in the actual design of the factory. Thus there remains the question of the degree to which the worker was happier in such conditions. Allan Nevins characterizes the lighting at Highland Park as "superb" and logically concludes that this made for greater safety. He also notes that "Highland Park offered superior working conditions."[37] However, the actual effect of the design in terms of the worker's contentment remains elusive for two reasons: First, few people bothered to ask the worker what he thought about it (few even asked him about the five-dollar day, when the opinion of just about everyone else was making news). Second, the workers' happiness was and is inextricably involved in a number of matters that have little to do with architecture. If at Highland Park the worker's contentment rested on architectural conditions alone, we might reasonably conclude that he would have been happier there than in other circumstances, but other considerations tended to mask any architecturally derived benefits. His happiness, for example, was apparently also related to Ford's avoidance of piecework, a degree of variety in the routine, the sense of being part of a popular manufacturing effort, and the five-dollar wage when that came along; his unhappiness would have sprung from the increased quotas noted previously, perhaps from the Sociological Department's paternal supervision, and, depending on the individual, other more subtle variables. In any case we have the obvious facts about the effects of Kahn's architecture on the user: better light, fewer columns, a cleaner floor, more even temperatures, and so forth, seem likely to have contributed to higher morale. But beyond these factors we can make only judgmental conclusions, unsubstantiated by hard data. What needs to be done, by both the historian and the designer, is to clarify the variables. Thus it would be useful to be able to isolate the variable of light, for example, or ventilation, in order to deal with its effect independent of the influences of wages, social policy, home life, production pace, and so forth. But this has not yet been done and certainly was not done in the industrial world of Kahn's time. Robert Sommer's recent book, *Personal Space*,[38] presents a useful methodology for doing this in some specific instances, but his methodology needs to be extended to other areas, perhaps to factories above all.

The Packard Forge Shop

Kahn also continued to enlarge the Packard factory. By 1910 the facilities had increased to some three or four times their 1905 size, most of the additions being repetitive units similar to Building Number Ten. An overview of the complex was illustrated in the *American Architect* of June 14, 1911. The same article illustrated a new forge shop for the plant, which broke sharply from the typical Packard format. An exterior photograph, two interiors, and a sectional drawing were again published in the *American Architect* of July 3, 1918, with a short accompanying article. Unlike its neighboring buildings, it was of one story only and could therefore appropriately be executed in steel, which was by then available in a wide variety of shapes at competitive cost.

It was an amazing structure. The remarkable sectional drawing is shown in figure 18. The crux of the problem was the provision of a ten-ton craneway 38 feet wide along the center of a column-free 72-foot-wide hall. The main trusses, placed at 15-foot intervals, spanned from column to column but carried the craneway suspended from their second interor panel points;[39] thus the crane was literally suspended over space, with no supports beneath the zone of its operation. Of course, one could easily argue that there are more direct ways to support a crane across a 72-foot void; one obvious example is simply to make the crane beam itself 70 feet or so in length. Such solutions would be simpler and were later used by Kahn. Nevertheless, one cannot avoid being caught up in the inventive virtuosity of this one-of-a-kind building. A triangular secondary truss gave lateral stability against wind loads and crane intertia by developing a rigid connection with the supporting columns. Longitudinal stresses from the same sources were resisted by intermittent X bracing in vertical planes. One interesting result of the configuration of the enclosing envelope was that the total wall height available for light and ventilation exceeded the height of the building itself. Expressed in terms of the total building height, 52 percent of the wall could be opened for ventilation and 70 percent was glazed. Equally interesting are the lines drawn to indicate paths of light and ventilation. They do not seem to be entirely scientific or accurate, since the lines indicating natural light were apparently simply drawn to connect the glass areas with points arbitrarily spaced equidistant across the floor, but they provide unarguable evidence of Kahn's conscious concern for those qualities and of at least a protoscientific attempt to analyze them. His imagination and ability have seldom appeared more brilliantly than in this sectional drawing.

Judged from the photographs, the resultant light quality was excellent (see fig. 19). All windows and louvers shown in section ran continuously through 23 bays from one end of the building to the other with only the slightest interruption by columns and trusses, presaging the continuous horizontal runs of fenestration of Kahn's later factories (fig. 17).

Office Structure and Organization

In addition to Packard, Pierce, and Ford, the office clientele between 1908 and 1916 included a great number of other industrial firms. Major factories were designed for Chalmers Motor Company, Dodge Brothers, Hudson Car Company, Lozier Motor Company, B. F. Goodrich Rubber Company, Joseph Mack Printing Company, and Continental Motor Car Company, all of Detroit; Bates Manufacturing Company of Lewiston, Maine; and the Industrial Works of Bay

Figure 17
Packard Motor Car Company Forge
Shop, Detroit, 1911; exterior. Note
the continuous horizontal runs of
glass and louvers bypassing the
structure as a curtain wall; compare
with the earlier Packard Plant
(figure 6). (Photograph courtesy of
American Architect and Building News.)

Figure 18
Packard Forge Shop; section showing
structure with paths of light and air
circulation indicated. (Photograph
courtesy of *American Architect and
Building News*.)

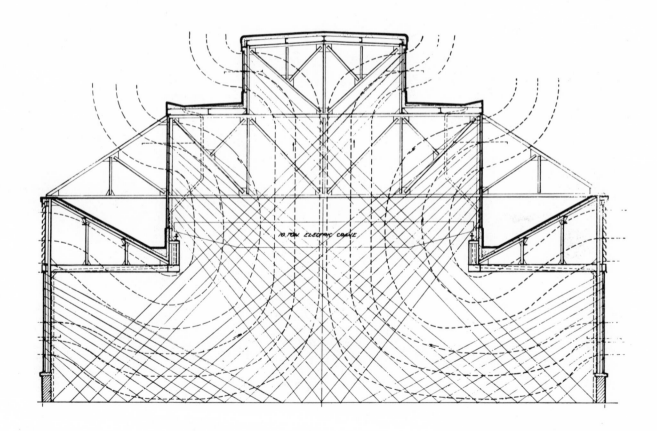

City, Michigan. The Bates factory was similar to Pierce, the Industrial Works was a simplified version of the Packard Forge Shop, and the others were generally multistory schemes of reinforced-concrete construction, of which the Hudson and Dodge plants were remarkably clear expressions. Perhaps because of the Dodge brothers' association with Ford, the Dodge plant was very similar to the Ford scheme, especially in its location of the administration building and the power house, but was largely devoid of the vestigial ornamentation.

The Kahn office grew accordingly. Albert's brother Louis (1886–1945) joined the firm in 1910 and remained permanently, later assuming an executive role second only to Albert. The total staff by 1910 consisted of some forty persons representing capabilities in pertinent branches of engineering as well as architecture, and Albert continued to associate with his brother Julius's firm for design of concrete structures. The role of Ernest Wilby in these early years has been a matter of some difference of opinion. The consensus among the most knowledgeable members of the present firm (who admittedly were not there during Wilby's tenure) is that he was responsible for the more purely visual elements of the design work. The corner towers and the cornice of the Ford Highland Park Plant are thought to have been by him, but he is believed to have had relatively little to do with the less ornamented Packard and Pierce plants or with decisions regarding structure and planning. That evaluation tends to be supported, though by no means proven, by two observations: first, Wilby's initialing of working drawing sheets is most often found with relation to elevations and ornamental details; and second, the development of factory solutions follows a straight-line evolution through the time of Wilby's departure from the office in 1922. Against this interpretation one must set the possibility that Wilby brought from his Yorkshire background a sense of the great potential of industrial architecture. If this was in fact the case, then his contribution must be regarded as a major one indeed. Further resolution of the question does not seem possible.

In 1907 Albert and Julius had designed the Trussed Concrete Building on Lafayette Avenue; on its completion Albert established his office on the top floor. By 1915 this space had become

Figure 19
Packard Forge Shop; interior.
(Photograph courtesy of *American Architect and Building News*.)

inadequate, and he began planning new quarters on the top floor of the Marquette Building in downtown Detroit. These were occupied in 1918.

> The various departments occupy approximately 14,000 feet of floor space. . . . There are two large drafting rooms, separate structural and mechanical engineering rooms, one for the specification writers and a separate room for the typing and assembling of specifications, chief superintendent's office and field superintendent's room, estimating room for contractors, two filing rooms for contracts, correspondence, etc. . . . The mechanical engineering department is at one extreme corner. The grouping of contractor's space for estimating, the accounting department, and the chief superintendent's office, as well as the office for field superintendents, works out particularly well. It brings these closely related departments into easy communication with one another. . . .
>
> All departments have graphical progress reports on their work. At the beginning of any work the estimated progress is indicated by a curve in black ink on co-ordinate paper, and the actual progress recorded from day to day in red ink. Any marked divergence in these curves indicates serious delay, and daily inspection of the records enables prompt action to be taken to remove it. The superintendent reports his progress in this way and also by means of daily and weekly reports. Thus a general and detailed supervision of all work is possible from the executive offices.[40]

Eighteen different paperwork forms were used for job records, not including general records and interoffice communications. These forms were similar to those used by the Ford Motor Company in its operation at Highland Park. The entire organization of the work process described here, in fact, recalls the automobile industry's "complex system for charting stock inventory, the transfer of materials, job routing, and the precise state of each assembly-line at a given moment."[41] Kahn was drawing organizational lessons from the industry he served.

Thus the office, which had grown to eighty people, was resettled, with its internal planning related to the flow pattern of work, a businesslike tracking of job progress, and a growing collection of skills and talents vested in an increasing number of key personnel. This last quality was reflected in the new letterhead, which replaced the former "Albert, Architect, Ernest Wilby, Associate":

ALBERT KAHN

J.R.BOYDE
WM.C.BUNCE
F.A.FAIRBROTHER
H.G.KNAPP
W.C.ROWLAND

ERNEST WILBY   LOUIS KAHN
J.F.HIRSCHMAN   ASSOCIATES

ARCHITECTS & ENGINEERS
MARQUETTE BUILDING
DETROIT, MICHIGAN

J.T.N.HOYT
CHIEF STRUCTURAL ENGINEER
F.K.BOOMHOWER
CHIEF MECHANICAL ENGINEER

Kahn in the Context of
His Contemporaries

If in 1903, when Kahn began his work with Packard, he had been more or less alone in his eagerness to try the factory as an architectural problem, a decade later he was not. By then his interest had been paralleled by that of a number of his contemporaries both at home and abroad. Frank Lloyd Wright with his usual perception had seen the potential of technological society. He had spoken on the machine on several occasions and was one of the first Oak Park, Illinois, residents to own a motorcar. In 1905 he had, in fact, done the E-Z Shoe Polish Factory in Chicago. This was a concrete structure like Kahn's Packard Building Number Ten of the same year, but it had brick-clad columns projecting outward from brick-clad spandrels to establish a simple, elegant rhythm on the facades. Wright's grasp of technological potential, however, which in its own way was superb,[42] was usually employed in the service of projects richer in poetic possibilities. For him, the E-Z Shoe Polish Factory was only a digression. But between 1904 and 1914, in Europe particularly, enthusiasm for the mechanistic and technological aspects of design was expressed by a growing number of architects. This enthusiasm formed the basis of the modern movement, and as such it bears discussion here, though its inclination toward the symbolic and theoretical rather than the pragmatic and practical distinguished it from Kahn's work and did so increasingly as time went on.

By 1904, the French architect Tony Garnier, an exact contemporary of Kahn, had drawn his vision of an imaginary Cité Industrielle, which for him represented a bold departure. He was of solidly Beaux-Arts training and had won the Rome Prize of 1899 with a national bank scheme that epitomized the tradition of academic composition. As might be expected, his academic background revealed itself in the Cité in a number of ways, and industry received much less attention than the title of the project implies. Furthermore, because the site was so ideally abstract, it avoided a number of the pressing issues that confront actual planning for an industrial metropolis. The Cité's great importance lies in the simple forward-looking architecture of the individual buildings and in the fact that the scheme as a whole, by an academician, did consider industry to be a part of the modern world and thus worthy of design attention.

The next European of importance in a related kind of design was Auguste Perret, five years younger than Kahn and, like Garnier, Ecole trained. His inclusion here depends on his garage in the Rue Ponthieu, Paris, of 1906. This is a building whose reinforced-concrete structure is left completely exposed. But for all its very direct appearance, the garage is not simply a result of internal and structural requirements as is Kahn's Packard building. The facade shows considerable subtle study, from the mathematical relationships between bays to the rose window and the obviously sophisticated window details elsewhere. Like Garnier, Perret attempted to modify an established academic and formal tradition to make it useful for an up-to-date building type and material.

The work of Peter Behrens requires the most lengthy discussion for a number of reasons: he was only one year older than Kahn; like Kahn, he probably would not have attained architectural greatness without industrial patronage; and his work and that of his immediate predecessor, Alfred Messel, were admired by Kahn. Behrens's background was in decorative Art Nouveau work. He became an architect after designing his own house at Darmstadt in 1900–1901. In 1907 he was hired as corporate designer for Allgemeine Electrizitäts Gesellschaft, the German General Electric Company. His most famous work is the A.E.G. Turbinenfabrik in Berlin, of 1908–1909, of combined concrete and steel construction. This great hall for the assembly of turbines was a long, column-free space 75 feet wide, 90 feet in total height, with a craneway running the full length, and with provision for further swinging cranes along the side wall. The structure was a three-hinged steel arch that described a roof profile of six facets resembling a gambrel roof. Over the central facets a doubly pitched skylight was erected so that the actual roof section approximated a gable. Side walls were glazed from a low sill right up to the cornice line. The corners of the structure, however, were massive concrete forms with horizontal lines inscribed at intervals, suggesting masonry rustication. At the ends, the faceted arch profile is used as the upper limit of a pedimentlike form that caps the building much in the manner of a classic temple.

This templelike quality has given rise to both praise and criticism—praise because of its bold vitality and expressive force, criticism because, in Reyner Banham's words, "the management of the massively rusticated and battered corners seems to make nonsense of the frame-and-fill and glass-and-steel structure of the sides."[43] It is fair to say of this building that while it provided a working assembly hall with due provision for programmatic needs, most decisions on the particular development of the envelope were made with a primary view to their expressive purpose. Stanford Anderson sums up Behrens's intentions and the significance of this building thus: "Beyond mere utility, Behrens sought to create the monuments and temples of a culture based on modern industrial power . . . both physical and corporate power. That Behrens intended this, and so fully achieved it, was what made his turbine factory unprecedented."[44] Behrens's later buildings do not entirely follow the pattern of the Turbinenfabrik. Indeed, some later assembly halls for A.E.G., in their simpler and more planar cladding, suggest a diaphanous enclosure similar to that of Kahn's steel-framed factory work. Behrens never completely abandoned the temple form and often turned to brick as a cladding material. Thus, in spite of their great size and powerful geometry, his buildings retain a suggestion of softness and romanticism.

Though it owed some minor formal debts to the Turbinenfabrik, the Fagus Shoe-last Factory at Alfeld an der Liene, which Walter Gropius and Adolph Meyer designed between 1911 and 1913, is based on a quite different expressive concept. Much of this factory is of massive, brick-clad, neoclassic forms. It owes its fame to one portion only, the proto-Bauhaus three-story workshop block. This block has a light brick base, the brick also being used to cover the columns, which batter inward as do the walls of the Turbinenfabrik. The glass and steel infill between columns minimizes the visual interruptions of the two intermediate floors because their edges are treated as much like the glass as possible by keeping the facing panels the same size and painting them dark. The entry at the end is a brick mass with striations that recall the corner treatment of the Turbinenfabrik. But the corner of the workshop block proper is very different and is the most original feature of the entire complex. No column occurs there, thus permitting the glass and the glasslike edges of the floors to meet at the corner in the lightest possible way. Finally, the entire block is firmly capped by a brick fascia recalling, and relating to, the brick base. The workshop has been considered the first building of the modern movement, presumably because of its bold and remarkably unromantic expression of forms uniquely possible in its time. Unlike Behrens, however, Gropius and Meyer were expressing, not the power of the technological age, but rather, presumably, the delicate ease with which new materials could generate new space-enclosing forms.

It should be clear that these men saw the challenge of industrial architecture in a frame of reference quite different from that of Kahn. They saw it in essentially artistic terms and were profoundly concerned with making it the standard-bearer for a new message about architecture's formal potential. By contrast, it would be extremely difficult to argue that Kahn's work for Packard, for example, takes formal or expressive considerations into account at all. In Wright's E-Z factory verticals predominate over horizontals for compositional reasons. In the Fagus factory the roof is treated differently from floors in order to give the floors a weightless quality and bring the composition to crisp resolution at the roof line. For Kahn such matters were subsidiary to a thorough grasp of practical considerations. Thus, as the conscious spokesman of an expressive concept, he is outclassed by the other men. The only elements of his early factories that were undoubtedly intended as artistic features were such things as the corner "towers" and cornice of the Ford plant. These were probably detailed by Wilby at Kahn's direction. They are artistic lightweights by comparison with Behrens's handling of a similar corner condition, or indeed by comparison with the airy statement of a new technological age found in the Fagus factory, or the dignified rhythm established by the projected piers of Wright's factory. The other men were, of course, consciously seeking aesthetic effects; they had been steeped in traditions that emphasized the artistic significance of architecture. With Wright this point is well established, as it is for

Gropius. Even in the 1920s, Gropius's Bauhaus Proclamation carried appeals to craftsmanship, spirituality, even "the Grace of Heaven [which causes] handicrafts to blossom into art."[45] Behrens's attitude toward the factory, previously summarized in Anderson's comment about the Turbinenfabrik, is exemplified by the evident and consistent monumentality of his buildings. Kahn, too, made reference to what he called the architectural merit (meaning aesthetic merit) of the factory, which strongly suggests that at the conscious level of public utterance he felt that the term "architecture" carried a necessary aesthetic connotation. But he did not insist that in factory design it was a necessarily premeditated concern or that it was the real reason for the architect's involvement.

The problems [of plant design] as a rule give scope for constructive thinking and planning, afford opportunity for exercising sound judgement in arrangement and, last but not least, for attractive grouping and external treatment. In regard to the latter, it is proven that a straightforward attack of the problem, the direct solution generally applied, that avoidance of unnecessary ornamentation, simplicity and proper respect for cost of maintenance, make for a type which, though strictly utilitarian and functional, has distinct architectural merit.[46]

Finally, mention must be made of the Futurists, the young Milanese visionaries whose experiences, also contrasting with Kahn's, help us to place him in a clearer light. In late 1908 or early 1909, Filippo Marinetti and a group of friends, sitting through the night in a Milan flat, became intoxicated by the contrast between the tramways to the front of the apartment and the canal behind—the dramatic symbolic juxtaposition, as it seemed to them, of past and future. They knew which appealed to them, and as dawn broke, they embarked on a wild chase in a great racing car, a "snorting [beast]," until finally, as recounted in the Foundation Manifesto, there came the revelation: "a roaring racing car . . . is more beautiful than the Winged Victory of Samothrace."[47] These may have been words to give birth to an age, but the Futurists designed no executed architecture at all. Their legacy is a series of exciting drawings, primarily by Antonio Sant'Elia, of visionary structures—skyscrapers intersected by multilevel roadways, airstrips, elevator shafts, overhead bridges resembling conveyors—*Dinamismo Architettònico*, to use Sant'Elia's term. On the very day these men were off in their racing car Kahn probably was busy at the more prosaic task of designing the Model T factory for Ford. While they were describing and delineating their visionary physical world, he was, if not building it, at least on the way to building it.

Why was Kahn's approach so rich in possibilities? Perhaps the reason can be found by turning again to some specifics of these early buildings. The Packard Forge Shop abandoned all reference to neoclassical temple forms, as Behrens's programmatically and dimensionally similar work did not. The interest that the Packard scheme has for design through concentration on mechanistic inventiveness, as in the suspended craneway and the light and ventilation possibilities, arose precisely from this ability to investigate a new form that was quite devoid of all ties to forms of conscious symbolic value. Gropius, Behrens, the Futurists, the German Expressionist architect Eric Mendelsohn (in such sketches as his car-body factory of 1914)—all reveal a concern for a finite, compositionally complete design. The Packard Forge Shop reflects no apparent thought for its compositional body and, consequently, no apparent concern for terminus; that is, the edges of the building have not been given any aesthetic treatment intended to bring the composition to a visual close or resolution. This is, perhaps, still more evident in the Ford Highland Park Plant, where, in spite of the vestigial corner towers, it is the individual bay, and not the building as a whole, that is clearly the crucial design unit. This was in part a result of the dynamic nature of the industry and the particular manufacturer for which Kahn was designing. In contrast to Garnier's, Sant'Elia's, or Mendelsohn's visionary sketches for imaginary clients, or Behrens's work for a relatively stable industry, Kahn's work was with a real client who was centrally concerned with growth and expansion. In such a situation, where a concern about the building's compositional terminus was nonsense, a serious architectural investigation was forced to pay attention, not to a building's composition in toto, but rather to the constituents of a typical cell, which might then be repeated in indeterminate extension. And indeed monumentality per se must have seemed frivolous in a situation where the entire plant might be outmoded in a decade, as indeed Highland Park was. Thus the Futurists' cry for the "constant renewal of the architectonic environment [where] our houses will last less time than we do"[48] was for Kahn an everyday reality requiring architectural comprehension and provision. So, too, the urge toward a crisp geometry found in Gropius and other Europeans may have grown from the Futurist position that "the straight line will be alive and palpitating; will lend itself to all the expressive necessities of our material, and its basic bare severity will be a symbol of the metallic severity of the lives of modern machinery."[49] But for Kahn the straight line was not palpitating, or expressive, or symbolic, except as a consequence of other factors. When he used it, he did so because it meant easier setting-out of the work on the site, fewer detail complications, simpler formwork, no specially cast bricks, and so on. His work was more analogous to the actual turbine, racing car, or shoe-last machinery than to the Europeans' consciously symbolic interpretation of any one of these.

Notes

1. Quoted in Helen Bennett, "Albert Kahn Gives People What They Want," original ms for an article prepared in June 1929 for *American Magazine*. The ms is in the files of the Kahn office.

2. W. Hawkins Ferry, *The Buildings of Detroit: A History* (Detroit: Wayne State University Press, 1968), p. 264, attributes this library to Kahn alone.

3. In 1922 Wilby, after twenty years with the Kahn office, went to the University of Michigan to teach, where he remained until his retirement in 1943. See Walter A. Donnelly, ed., *The University of Michigan—an Encyclopedic Survey*, Vol. 3 (Ann Arbor: University of Michigan Press, 1953), p. 1303, which states that "He was an outstanding faculty figure. . . ."

4. The name of the firm was later changed to the Truscon Steel Company with Julius as president. He became a vice-president of Republic Steel when that company purchased Truscon. The Truscon trade name is now used by the Great Lakes Cement Tile Division of the Brown-McLaren Manufacturing Company.

5. An article on Albert and Julius appeared in the *Detroit News Tribune* on Sunday, September 20, 1908, and some portions are of interest here. In describing the brothers, the article said, "One saw the poetry in life, the embellishments and the beauties; the other saw the structural backbone, the practical relations of concrete things. Julius Kahn is the young engineer who . . . has revolutionized building, and has made it possible to erect a 20 story skyscraper with a poured concrete skeleton. . . . Albert Kahn, is primarily the artist, the man whose interest is in the hitherto ugly lines of concrete. . . ."

6. Brief biographies of both James F. and Henry B. Joy can be found in Clarence M. Burton, *The City of Detroit* (Detroit-Chicago: S. J. Clarke Publishing Co., 1922), Vol. 3; see pp. 5–7 and 94–99.

7. This date has been a matter of some controversy. Glenn A. Niemeyer, *The Automotive Career of Ransom E. Olds* (East Lansing: Michigan State University, 1963), the most authoritative work on Olds, claims to have traced the bill of lading, which was dated in the spring of 1893. The car was shipped to the Bombay, India, office of the Francis Times Company of London but was lost in transit.

8. John K. Barnes, "The Romance of our Automobile Makers," *World's Work* 49 (April 1921): 564; quoted in Niemeyer, *Olds*, p. 48.

9. Niemeyer, *Olds*, p. 37.

10. This plant was once thought to have been the first factory of reinforced concrete built in this country, the assumption being that it was done in 1903, the year of Kahn's retention by Joy as architect for Packard. It is now known that the building dates from 1905 and follows the nine earlier mill construction factories. Thus, Packard Plant Number Ten is later than Ernest Ransome's reinforced-concrete factories in the East and is, in fact, contemporary with Frank Lloyd Wright's concrete E-Z Shoe Polish Factory. See Ada Louise Huxtable, "Factory for Packard Motor Car Company—1905." *Progressive Architecture* 38 (October 1957): 121–122.

11. Ferry, *Buildings of Detroit*, p. 181, notes a length of 457 feet. The 322-foot dimension appears repeatedly on plans of the Packard Complex up to 1915. As of that date the total depth of the block, front to back, was only 386 feet.

12. See Leonard K. Eaton, "Frame of Steel," *Architectural Review* 126 (November 1959): 289–290.

13. Stirrups are lengths of reinforcing bar stock bent into a stirrup or U shape and placed vertically within the beam to resist a tendency for the beam to fracture along a series of planes at 45 degrees to its axis.

14. Continuity refers to the characteristic common to concrete structures in which a beam or girder is continued across a support without a joint or interruption. This is a useful structural treatment, resulting in greater overall efficiency, but it means that the stresses within the beam, in the area of the support, are opposite to those conventionally found in a beam that simply spans a void in the more usual manner. In particular, a beam used in the usual way will be compressed along its top surface and stretched along the bottom, while a beam used in continuity will, over its supports, be stretched along its top surface and compressed along the bottom.

15. For a useful and more detailed tracing of the history of reinforced concrete, see Carl Condit, "The First Reinforced-Concrete Skyscraper . . . ," *Technology and Culture* 9, No. 1 (January 1969): 1–12.

16. See Ada Louise Huxtable, "Reinforced-Concrete Construction," *Progressive Architecture* 38, No. 9 (September 1957): 139–142.

17. See note 13, this chapter.

18. Bonding of the steel bar to the surrounding concrete is necessary simply to prevent the bar from slipping. Steel reinforcing bar material is commonly "deformed" (fabricated with bumps) to aid bonding, but the ends of bars also are commonly bent into hook shapes for greater security against slipping. This creates a mechanical hooking action but also, by prolonging the bar's length, brings more of the steel surface into contact with the surrounding concrete. Because the length of the Kahn bar's shear reinforcing wings was limited as described in the text, the length available for hooking was insufficient.

19. The booklet is entitled *The Typical Factory: The Factory Behind the Car*, printed in Detroit by the Joseph Mack Printing House and copyrighted 1907 by the Trussed Concrete Steel Company. The known copy is held by Mrs. Malbin. Other copies may exist, though none are in the files of Albert Kahn Associates Inc., Architects and Engineers, nor is the factory mentioned in any other publications of the work of either that firm or Lockwood, Greene and Company (but see note 22). The booklet deals exclusively with the Pierce Plant. The Pierce Plant, now owned by the Larry Commercial Corporation, still exists but has been much remodeled and is now occupied by a number of concerns. All information herein refers to the original scheme as presented in the booklet.

20. *The Typical Factory*, pp. 5–6. The year to which these monthly dates refer is not given directly, but on p. 23 a letter from Lockwood, Greene and Company to the Trussed Concrete Steel Company is reproduced, referring to "the Kahn system of reinforced concrete, which was used in the construction of the new factory for the Geo. N. Pierce Company at Buffalo, New York. . . ." This letter is dated February 25, 1907, and thus fixes the year of construction as 1906.

21. For examples of the work of Lockwood, Greene and Company see *American Architect*, Vol. 109, No. 2100 (March 22, 1916): 193, 195 (the earliest Avery listing of work by that firm); Vol. 118, No. 2344 (November 24, 1920): 675–677; Vol. 123, No. 2420 (May 23, 1923): 465–470; Vol. 126, No. 2461 (December 17, 1924): 589–590.

22. Six plates of drawings (no photographs) of the Administration Building alone appear in *American Architect* 91, No. 1636 (May 4, 1907), the architect of that portion of the complex being given as George Cary. No mention of him appears in the booklet by the Trussed Concrete Steel Company, though that booklet discusses the construction of an Administration Building identical to Cary's drawings, and no mention of the Trussed Concrete Steel Company, Albert Kahn, or Lockwood, Greene and Company appears with the drawings in *American Architect*. The issue is devoted exclusively to reinforced concrete in architecture and is a useful reference on the state of the technique at that time.

23. The term *monitor* as related to factories refers to a superstructure with glazed sides, projecting upward from the roof to provide natural light to the interior of the building. A monitor differs from a skylight in that glazing occurs in vertical or near-vertical surfaces and differs from a clerestory in that no wall occurs underneath. A sawtooth roof consists of a series of single-faced monitors placed side by side to form the roof of the building.

24. *The Typical Factory*, p. 10.

25. An interesting note appears regarding column size: "the interior columns are 14 by 14 inches reinforced with four ¾ inch by 2 inch Kahn bars; the exterior 16 by 16, with the same reinforcement. The size of the exterior columns is increased by these dimentions [sic] for architectural affect" (*The Typical Factory*, p. 16.) The 16 by 16-inch column was probably required for the Garage to carry the loading due to the larger spans and was used in the Brazing Building possibly for consistency but probably to permit repetitive sash on the same column module. Architectural effect is a value that finds precious little emphasis elsewhere in the booklet, and on several occasions the design criterion is made unmistakably clear: "In every instance the most economical method or material, from the standpoint of results, is employed. Where structural steel proved the cheapest, structural steel was used; where brick was cheapest, brick was used; where reinforced concrete was cheapest, reinforced concrete was used . . ." (ibid., p. 6).

26. Ibid., p. 18.

27. Ibid., p. 16.

28. Concrete trusses including Vierendeel types were used for 60-foot spans in the Terminal Station, Atlanta, Georgia, of 1903–1904; see Condit, "The First Reinforced-Concrete Skyscraper," pp. 27–28. Whether either of the Kahns was aware of this building is not known.

29. *The Typical Factory*, p. 6.

30. Ford's anti-Semitism is a matter of historical record, but as with many of Ford's strongly stated positions it was subject to wide variations in individual circumstances. For example, after attacks on the Jews (published in the *Dearborn Independent*), Ford's old friend and neighbor Rabbi Leo M. Franklin appeared noticeably cool, and Ford inquired, "What's wrong, Dr. Franklin? Has something come between us?" Allan Nevins and Frank Ernest Hill, *Ford, Expansion and Challenge: 1915–1932* (New York: Scribners, 1957), p. 315; see also pp. 311–323.

31. Horace L. Arnold and Fay L. Faurote, *Ford Methods and the Ford Shops* (New York: the Engineering Magazine Company, 1919), is an exhaustive coverage of operations at Highland Park.

32. Bennett, "Albert Kahn Gives People What They Want," p. 17.

33. See Allan Nevins and Frank Ernest Hill, *Ford, the Times, the Man, and the Company* (New York: Scribners, 1954), p. 453.

34. Ibid., p. 454.

35. Ibid., p. 577. This attitude could have its harmful side (see Nevins and Hill, *Ford, Expansion*, pp. 508ff), though the blame cannot possibly be laid on the design of the buildings.

36. Nevins and Hill, *Ford, the Times*, p. 550.

37. Ibid., p. 537.

38. Robert Sommer, *Personal Space* (Englewood Cliffs, N.J.: Prentice-Hall, 1969).

39. The panel points of a truss are the points on the upper and lower members—chords—at which vertical or diagonal members are connected.

40. George C. Baldwin, "The Offices of Albert Kahn, Architect, Detroit, Michigan," *Architectural Forum* 29, No. 5 (November 1918): 125–130.

41. Nevins and Hill, *Ford, the Times*, pp. 450–451.

42. See Reyner Banham, *Architecture of the Well-Tempered Environment* (Chicago: University of Chicago Press, 1969).

43. Reyner Banham, *Theory and Design in the First Machine Age* (London: Architectural Press, 1960), p. 83.

44. Stanford Owen Anderson, "Peter Behrens and the New Architecture of Germany, 1900–1917," Doctoral thesis, Columbia University (Fine Arts), 1968.

45. As quoted by Banham, *Theory and Design*, p. 277.

46. As quoted by W. Hawkins Ferry, *The Legacy of Albert Kahn* (Detroit: Detroit Institute of Arts, 1970), p. 165.

47. As quoted in Banham, *Theory and Design*, pp. 101, 103.

48. Ibid., p. 135.

49. Ibid., p. 121.

4
EARLY NONINDUSTRIAL VENTURES, 1896–1916

Smaller Projects

In the years from 1903 to 1910 Kahn continued to do residential commissions. Representative of a number of them is the house he built for himself at 208 Mack Avenue in Detroit in 1906 (now the Detroit Urban League). It is two stories high, with a dormered hipped roof and a brick and stucco exterior with the second-floor line indicated by a string course. It has a two-story projecting window bay placed asymmetrically and a segmental porch roof.[1] The Holt and Sloman houses in Detroit are similar designs, as are, on a more elaborate scale, the Delta Upsilon fraternity house in Ann Arbor and Cranbrook House in Bloomfield Hills. All are from the period 1905–1910. Completely different, however, is the house that Kahn designed in 1908 for Henry Joy on Lake Shore Road in Grosse Pointe (fig. 20). Now demolished, this was a very direct, orderly, and restrained two-story brick structure with a purely rectangular central portion and wings to either side. The treatment was austere. The building depended for its effect on the purely architectural values of materials and massing, with precise openings for light and air. Its ancestor was the Watson Freer house of 1895, but in the Joy house Kahn used even less ornament, reducing the composition to the simplest and most direct terms. His attitude toward this house is interesting; he saw it, not as an exercise in residential elegance, but as "a study in mass and space."[2] For the Detroit Golf Club design of 1917, also executed in brick, he used a similarly restrained approach with slightly more picturesque massing.

The University of Michigan: Hill Auditorium

In 1903 Kahn had designed the Engineering Building (now West Engineering Building) for the University of Michigan. L-shaped in plan to suit its corner location and three stories high with hipped roofs, it is not a particularly outstanding or innovative work. Its main feature is the arch at the corner forming the gateway to the campus Diagonal, flanked on the campus side by two neobaroque towers. Through time this has become the tradition-laden "Engine Arch" of the campus. The Engineering Building was a sound work, however, with usable and well-lighted interior loft spaces, and it formed a solid basis for Kahn's continuing relationship with the university. It is probable that the resultant commission for Arthur Hill Memorial Auditorium was awarded in 1910, since the drawings are dated October 5, 1911.

Hill Auditorium is one of Kahn's most interesting nonindustrial designs (fig s. 21–23). It is in many ways Sullivanian. The bold major opening punched into the vaultlike mass and the handling of ornament recall Sullivan's Getty Tomb or the Midwest banks (of which only that of Owatonna, Minnesota, had been completed at the time; the Owatonna Bank was published in detail in the *Architectural Record* of October 1908). The auditorium portion has been treated as a solid block executed in a rich, deeply toned brick. It is abutted by a smaller office and utilities block of the same material.[3] Marquees to either side are of ornamental metal fretted in a pattern that resembles the main cornice. The interior, too, has a Sullivanian overtone (see fig. 23), though it is more closely related to Sullivan's Garrick Theatre in the Schiller Building of 1891–1892.

The true authorship of the Hill scheme is not easy to determine. As with all office commissions of that time, it went out under the attribution "Albert Kahn, Architect, Ernest Wilby, Associate." The exterior and interior elevation drawings for the job are initialed as done by E.W., as is one detailing the lobby desk, though nearly all drawings are initialed as checked by A.K. The suggestion might be that Wilby was therefore responsible for the design. Yet the theme of mass and void counterplay is just the kind of thing to which Kahn's own abilities were so well suited and toward which many of his European photographs of the twenties would be oriented. In this respect Kahn's own predilections nicely meshed with Sullivan's formal inspiration. If in fact Kahn was the author of the design, another question follows: Why was the Hill theme never again used in Kahn's work? The answer may possibly be found in the growing unpopularity of Sullivan's concepts, as opposed to a growing acceptance of directions defined by McKim, Mead and White. For whatever Kahn's relationship to Sullivanian inspiration, his admiration for McKim was one of the beacons of his life. In any case, only a few of Kahn's other nonindustrial commissions come up to the quality of Hill Auditorium.

The design of Hill involved what must have been one of the most complete acoustical analyses to that time, for which Hugh Tallant as consulting acoustic engineer was largely responsible.[4]

Figure 20
Henry B. Joy residence, Detroit,
1908–1909 (now demolished). A
further development of the Freer
scheme of 1895. (Photograph by
Manning Bros.)

Figure 21
Arthur Hill Memorial Auditorium,
University of Michigan, Ann Arbor,
1910–1911; exterior. (Photograph by
Hedrich-Blessing, courtesy of Albert
Kahn Associates.)

Figure 22
Hill Auditorium, Ann Arbor; main
floor plan and section. (Photograph
courtesy of *American Architect and
Building News*.)

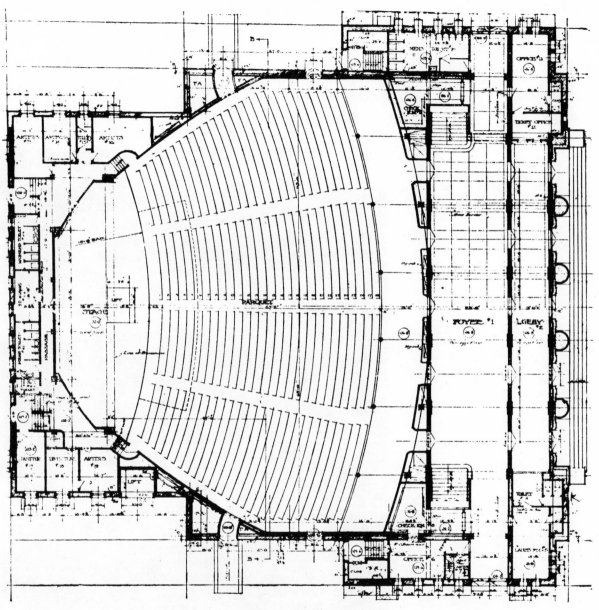

MAIN FLOOR PLAN

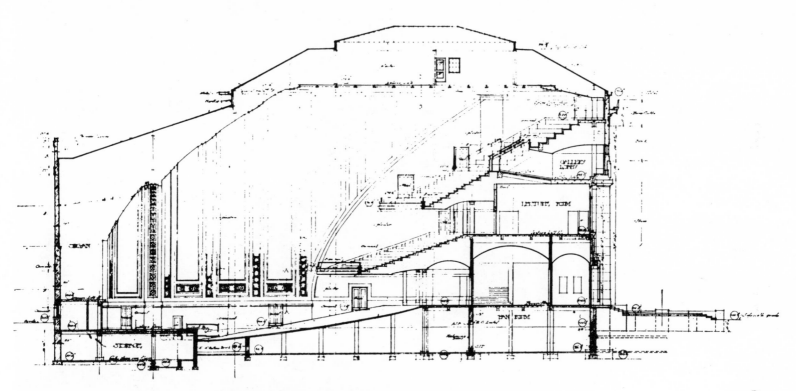

"LONGITUDINAL" SECTION "ON LINE A.A

Figure 23
Hill Auditorium, Ann Arbor;
interior. (Photograph by Manning
Bros., courtesy of Albert Kahn
Associates.)

Because Hill is a very large auditorium, seating nearly 5,000, the acoustics design was unusually challenging. The chief differences between this problem and that of the usual theater were

> First, . . . it was necessary to use not only the side walls and ceiling but also all of the wall and ceiling surfaces at the sides and to the rear of the platform. If this had not been done, a large part of the audience would not have received deflected sound but only the direct sound of the speaker's voice. Thus it was not possible to have a theatre or opera stage in this auditorium. . . .
>
> Second, the width of the platform . . . could not be increased in proportion to the greater number of seats although it would have been very desirable to do so. The reason for this was that the proper convergence of side walls and ceiling toward the platform could not be obtained with a wider platform than the one adopted, and echoes would have resulted due to the speaker's voice being deflected from the side wall near the stage to those sitting on the opposite side of the hall. . . .
>
> In the path from the reflected surface to the hearer the reflected sound does not decrease in intensity when reflected from a double curved surface. . . . This is why the ceiling and side walls were designed in the shape of a paraboloid of revolution. . . .
>
> Reflected sound . . . received by a hearer on the opposite side of the hall . . . would exceed the path of the direct sound by very much more than the limiting seventy feet, and therefore . . . the greater part of the hall is limited to one reflected sound. . . .
>
> To prevent any exterior sounds . . . the exterior wall, where the same also forms the wall of the auditorium proper, consists of a solid brick wall, a four-inch air space and a four-inch hollow tile interior wall. The roof of the building is covered with tile which prevents the sound of rain falling upon it from penetrating to the interior [a necessary consideration in Ann Arbor].[5]

The result is one of the finest acoustic spaces of its size in the country. Unlike many other auditoriums, Hill has never required any acoustical remodeling. The university has undergone tremendous growth since 1911, and the techniques of acoustic design are now better developed, but the auditorium still is more than adequate and has contributed greatly to the excellence of the school. Extracurricular amenities of large scale are economically feasible and of high acoustic quality.

The richly textured brick surfaces of Hill were used by Kahn repeatedly over the next several years in a series of buildings. Included in this series are the Science Building (now Natural Science Building) of 1917 and the General Library of 1919, both for the University of Michigan, and a group of buildings done in the late years of World War I for the U.S. Aviation School at Langley Field, Virginia. Oddly enough, the Langley Field brickwork is unusually fancy and interspersed with colored tile patterns.

Second European Trip

On December 2, 1911, Albert and Ernestine sailed for Europe. They landed first at Madeira, went ashore again for a day at Algiers, then went on to Italy, where they spent the major part of their tour. They landed at Genoa, as Albert had done alone in 1891, then went on to Naples, Pompeii, Amalfi, Palermo, Rome, Siena, Florence, Bologna, and Venice (fig. 24). Albert's sketches from the trip date from January 2 through January 21, when they left Italy to spend a few days around Paris. The sketches retain the nonpicturesque quality of the earlier drawings but show other differences. Most are of Renaissance palazzi, and other buildings drawn are well known, even commonplace. The Palazzo Vecchio, the Bargello, and the basilica of San Miniato al Monte in Florence are included in addition to the usual palazzi of that city; the basilica of San Zeno Maggiore at Verona was drawn, and the Torre del Mangia at Siena. Most of the drawings were done to a specified scale with a straightedge. By contrast with the sketches of 1891, the selection seems to have been less spontaneous and more conscious of current vogues. The two decades that separated the two trips had encompassed the heyday of the influence of McKim, Mead and White. Kahn's attitudes perhaps reflected that influence, to which he had, we recall, responded with great enthusiasm as early as 1893–1894.

The Detroit Athletic Club

He and Ernestine departed for the United States on February 7, 1912. He must have received the commission for the Detroit Athletic Club shortly after his return to Detroit. Henry Joy was instrumental in the refounding of the dormant club early in 1912. He was chosen vice-president and was probably influential in the selection of Kahn as architect for the building.

The solution was a six- and seven-story structure, constructed in 1914–1915, and still standing at 241 Madison Avenue in the heart of downtown Detroit (fig. 25). The inspiration for the design

Figure 24
Albert and Ernestine in the Piazza
San Marco, Venice, 1912.
(Photograph courtesy of Mrs. Martin
Butzel.)

is clear. It was executed in a rather freely interpreted Renaissance palazzo style in the manner of McKim, Mead and White, and it derived from Kahn's recent Italian tour and from McKim, Mead and White's own prototypal and magnificent University Club in New York of 1900. Kahn was proud of the Detroit Athletic Club; he said he had intended it to be his monument.

From 1903 to the time of this commission, his designs had been in large measure workable answers to problems of practical program need. When such problems did not exist to any degree, in the Joy house, for example, he seems almost to have invented goals whose pursuit might be relevant to the larger works. The Detroit Athletic Club, however, did not intrinsically possess such practical problems, and invention of goals for such a major work may well have seemed irresponsible and whimsical. Furthermore, in the context of the time, the nonpractical criterion of dignified elegance would have been stressed by the client if not by Kahn himself, and it was this criterion that undoubtedly led to the choice of stylistic treatment. This was Kahn's first major work in an identifiable period style, and the absence of a strong practical stimulus is to some extent regrettable. Kahn, of course, did not have McKim's lengthy and elaborate formal training, and certainly the Detroit Athletic Club does not have the irresistible elegance of McKim's University Club. Although much of the detail is quite fine, as a totality the building is lacking in vigor. The cornice and the horizontal string courses are weak in relation to the overall mass of the building, and the rustication and quoining are too restrained to provide relief. The entire facade, in fact, is rather two-dimensional. This quality is still more apparent in the interiors (fig. 27), where pilasters and moldings hardly free themselves from the general wall plane. This planarity is logical for Kahn's factories, but here in a period style it simply seems vapid, lacking the crisp vitality that distinguishes the Freer house or Hill Auditorium.

In another way, too, the Detroit Athletic Club is not up to the best of Kahn's nonindustrial work. McKim could generate magnificent interior volumes and attendant masses with brilliant skill. This quality was to be found in its most impressive form in the recently demolished Pennsylvania Station and is still impressive in the library of the University Club or Low Library

Figure 25
The Detroit Athletic Club, Detroit,
1913–1915; exterior. (Photograph by
Hedrich-Blessing, courtesy of Albert
Kahn Associates.)

Figure 26
The Detroit Athletic Club; entrance
detail. (Photograph by Hedrich-
Blessing, courtesy of Albert Kahn
Associates.)

at Columbia University. Kahn's McKim-like work, the Athletic Club included, is generally devoid of these magnificent volume-mass relationships. Kahn's great interior volumes significantly come from programmatic challenges; Hill Auditorium is one sort of example, the Packard Forge Shop, another.

In nonindustrial designs both during this period and later Kahn was clearly a conservative. So were many of his clients, and Kahn was thereby certainly more acceptable to them than a more avowedly liberal designer would have been. Leonard Eaton has recently provided a very interesting study of the clients of the radical Frank Lloyd Wright and the conservative Howard Van Doren Shaw, which sheds some light on the conservative side of Kahn's practice.[6] Eaton shows that Wright's clients tended to be tinkerers, inventors, and so forth, makers of things, while Shaw's clients tended to be men concerned with making money. By such an analysis Henry Ford stands out among Kahn's clients as of the first type. Ford was a prime sponsor of Kahn's revolutionary industrial work, but Kahn in his conservative hat did no nonindustrial work for Ford. Interestingly, Ford nearly had his house done by Wright, thereby choosing revolutionary design in both home and factory, though this does not help to explain Ford's own brand of conservatism. Otherwise, Kahn's clients can be classified as money-makers and businessmen, not inventors, and they were men of consistently conservative taste. Sponsorship of liberal or even revolutionary factory designs was clearly in their self-interest when the economics of such factories could be demonstrated, but when they wanted nonindustrial designs, they apparently requested conservative work. The client most difficult to categorize as either money-maker or inventor is, of course, the University of Michigan; in this connection it is interesting to note that many clients of the conservative Shaw had ties with the University of Chicago.

Kahn provided the conservative work as wanted, but this does not mean that he was merely pleasing or "selling" the client. He was, in fact, operating in a manner consistent with his earliest image of the architect, and above all he was working consistently with his image of McKim. It was a matter of simple coincidence that the tastes of his business and university clientele generally supported similar directions through the first third of the century.

In this same period Kahn did a number of large commercial buildings for downtown Detroit, including the already mentioned Trussed Concrete Building of 1907 (where he and Julius established their offices), the Palmer Building of 1910, the Ford Motor Company Service Building of 1913, the Detroit Free Press Building of the same year, and the Kresge Building of 1914. All but the last of these employed the familiar early twentieth-century commercial facade, consisting of a simple grid with glass infill capped by a decorative cornice. The Kresge Building differed because of its tall proportions, eighteen stories high by five bays wide, with an arcade and gable terminus. In 1910 Kahn also designed the neobaroque National Theatre on Monroe Street.

The "Farm," Walnut Lake

In 1914 Kahn began a summer home for his family at Walnut Lake, twenty miles northwest of Detroit. It burned before completion. However, rebuilding was begun with minor changes, and the house was finished early in 1917 (fig. 28).[7] The exterior follows the massing already used in the Freer and Joy houses, but the Walnut Lake house is divided into horizontal strata marked by the continuous trellis line over the lower-story windows and by the continuous sill line of the upper windows. Each window band is relatively continuous and uninterrupted by wall surface. On the main floor behind the windows of the main central mass lies a single large room linked to the flanking porches through very large openings. Kahn was aware of Wright's work, and Wright's predilection for designing in strata of fluid open spaces may have been of some influence here. The upper floor, however, is concisely compartmentalized; behind every third mullion of the central portion there lies a wall, dividing this portion into four equal rooms. Opposite these rooms, across a hall, are other bedrooms, toilets, and a stairway, also modularly planned and arranged symmetrically about the entrance-chimney axis. Kahn's attitude toward the design is again interesting; he intended this to be a design based on economy in the absolute sense, that is, direct and efficient use of materials and methods. The window treatment reflects this attitude as much as it does any Wrightian influence or formal consideration. Within each floor the window

detailing is repetitive. Between the window strata the horizontal boarding runs continuously with little need to accommodate itself to short runs of wall surface. This simplicity of fenestration would later be exploited by Kahn in factory design. There is also a plan of the garden plantings by his hand, but for much of this he was guided by Ernestine. The grounds themselves are extensive. The house lies some 200 yards south of the main road. South of the house itself is the formal garden shown in figure 28, and southeast of it, at a distance of perhaps 120 yards, is the shore of the small lake.

Ernestine and Albert used the Walnut Lake home as their summer residence for the rest of their lives, keeping the house in town as their permanent winter home. Rosalie, the youngest daughter, recalled an active household schedule both in town and at Walnut Lake.

Mother and Father entertained fairly often and were entertained frequently. I would say that they spent more time than average with their sisters and brothers . . . both came from good sized families and lots of the members lived in Detroit. We lived next door to one of Mother's sisters and her husband, and two doors away from one of her brothers and his family. Occasionally my parents played bridge with one of the couples. Neither of them were good players, but they were good-natured about the game. Father loved baseball and often went to see the Tigers play when they were in town. He also attended football games at Ann Arbor, and followed my brother's career with the University of Michigan varsity hockey team. He himself was not an active sportsman of any kind. *Once* he tried to learn to ride horseback, but he was a round, short-legged little man, and he almost rolled off. That was his first and last try.

. . . The family often went on tours of the east—New York and Boston, also Philadelphia; the children (Lydia, Edgar, Ruth and I) were taken to theatre, the opera, museums and historical sites. . . .

In my day there was the weekly concert of the Detroit Symphony during the winter season; . . . the record player was often used . . . for classical music only, when Father was at home. I don't know when or why Father stopped playing the piano . . . he was not willing to do anything to which he could not give his best effort; he had to choose, and architecture was it. I do know that he never set finger to a piano in my conscious lifetime. But he was just as absorbed in listening to music as in working. He would sit with his mouth open, apparently drinking in the sound more fully in this manner, and he would hardly move a muscle. At some particularly pleasing passage he would murmur to himself "Beautiful, beautiful." On Saturday afternoons he would come home to listen with Mother to the broadcast from the Met; these he seldom missed; they were his great relaxation and pleasure. . . .

Figure 28
Summer home of Albert Kahn, Walnut Lake (outside Detroit), 1914–1917. (Photograph courtesy of Mrs. Martin Butzel.)

He never came home at night when he knew he would be there for the evening without bringing plans to study and work over. At dinner he would bring my mother up to date on the events of the day. Immediately afterward he would take his "little nap" of 15 or 20 minutes, then jump up from the couch fully awake, and proceed to his "den" to immerse himself in his beloved work. He concentrated so hard that he would never notice if I sneaked in to watch him. . . .

In the summertime there was *croquet*, a little bridge, listening to music, but just as in the city, work went on in the den at the Farm too, almost every evening. There was never a summer that I remember spent anywhere but at Walnut Lake from I think 1917 or 18 on. Father drove himself to work and back every day and always felt refreshed at the very sight of the Farm, as it has always been called. He really loved it. Mother was the gardener in the family; whenever there were visitors they weren't allowed to sit down until they had walked through the gardens and shown proper appreciation. On Sundays there was an open invitation to our friends to come for supper. Edgar (then unmarried) would bring doctor friends or the current girl over from Ann Arbor. My sisters (and I when I got to that age) had friends who dropped in for a swim and stayed to play baseball on the Mall. I don't think there were ever less than 20 for buffet supper on Sunday nights.[8]

Notes

1. The *Architectural Review* referred to the style as "Ernest Newton-Georgian." Buford Pickens, "Treasure Hunting at Detroit," *Architectural Review* 96 (London: December 1944): 174.

2. Mrs. Malbin's recollection of his comment.

3. W. Hawkins Ferry, *The Buildings of Detroit: A History* (Detroit: Wayne State University Press, 1968), p. 189, states that the choice of brick was influenced by Kahn's observations in Bologna during his European trip of 1912. That would mean that the final brick choice was made while the building was under construction.

4. Tallant had published a series of articles on acoustics in *The Brickbuilder* 19, Nos. 5–12 (May–December 1910). He was retained by the Kahn office as acoustics consultant on the basis of the articles.

5. J. T. N. Hoyt, "The Acoustics of the Hill Memorial Hall, University of Michigan, Ann Arbor," *American Architect* 104, No. 1963 (August 6, 1913): 50–53.

6. Leonard K. Eaton, *Two Chicago Architects and Their Clients: Frank Lloyd Wright and Howard Van Doren Shaw* (Cambridge, Mass.: MIT Press, 1969).

7. The house appeared in *American Architect* 126, No. 2459 (November 19, 1924). The photographs taken then show the garden planting fully established.

8. Letter from Mrs. Butzel to the author, April 10, 1967.

5

THE FORD ROUGE PLANT AND RELATED PROJECTS, 1916–1932

The Impact of the Assembly Line

Henry Ford introduced the powered moving assembly line at Highland Park in 1913.[1] He did not invent it—it had previously been used for such operations as meat-packing—but he expanded it, refined it, and gave it an entirely new scale of application. The process hinged on moving the product-to-be by means of a powered continuous conveyance through the manufacturing stages, each of which was stationary. By comparison with the prior method of bringing the various operations to the product, or of moving the product by a noncontinuous process, the powered moving assembly line proved to be more efficient in its use of both men and machines. The technique was also essential for highly mechanized assembly because only in that way could the necessary numbers of large machines find adequate space and permanent anchorage. The process is commonly called mass production, but production in quantity is only one of its concerns. Ford summarized it as "the focussing upon a manufacturing operation of seven different principles: power, accuracy, economy, continuity, system, speed, and repetition."[2] It proved to be the key to efficient volume production.

The assembly line brought a change in factory design, for although it was used in the multistory Highland Park Plant, that was not the ideal architectural scheme for housing it. In a multistory building, the conveyor belt or chain can negotiate changes in level by ramping, but the ramped portion will normally be unavailable for assembly processes. If, on the other hand, the changes in level are accomplished by elevators, loading and unloading are required, and the elevator, which is an expensive piece of equipment, does not directly contribute to assembling the product. These inefficiencies are avoided by the one-floor scheme. Ford himself was one of the first to see this. As early as 1915 he was pondering a vast acreage of land on the Rouge River southwest of Detroit, on which extensive one-story units could be built . By 1923 Ernest Kanzler, a key Ford official in the area of production efficiency, could state a general Ford policy: "We had decided that multiple story buildings were not effective."[3]

The assembly line also affected plant design in another way. Most of Kahn's factory work before 1914 had been executed in reinforced concrete, but the particular advantages of concrete—

its fireproofness, its ability to damp vibration, and its imperviousness to corrosion or deterioration—are most important in multistory work. For a one-story building these attributes are less important; the question of vibration damping is usually of no importance whatsoever since the machines commonly rest on a surface that in turn rests directly on the earth. On the other hand, steel framing has certain advantages. Since it requires no formwork and no curing time, it has a potential superiority in speed of construction.[4] Furthermore, modular complexities in the layout of machines and conveyor systems are least aggravated if the spans are very large and the columns very small. For any given load the steel column will be smaller in plan dimensions, and, though concrete can be used for spans greater than the 40, 55, and 61 feet of Pierce, dead load becomes disproportionate for spans greater than 50 feet or so. With steel this problem is less severe. In view of Ford's conviction that the factory complex had to anticipate change, it should also be noted that steel construction somewhat simplifies problems of future remodeling and expansion. It is not surprising, therefore, that nearly all Kahn's work for Ford after 1915 was structured in steel.

Beginnings of the
Ford Rouge Complex:
The Eagle Plant

Kahn's first steel-frame building had been a simple one-story sawtooth-roofed plant for Burroughs Adding Machine Company, built on Second Avenue in Detroit in 1904.[5] He had used steel for the sawtooth-roofed machine shop for Ford at Highland Park and for the Packard Forge Shop of 1911. He was now to use steel for the immense Eagle Submarine Chaser Plant for Ford Motor Company.

Henry Ford had convinced the government that this proposed boat for world war antisubmarine work could be mass-produced like the Model T, with comparable economy and speed. On January 17, 1918, he was directed to proceed with the work, in cluding construction of a government-financed factory to build the boat. The plant was in operation by May of the same year and launched its first boat on July 10.

The site was not Highland Park but rather a 2,000-acre tract on the Rouge River near

Ford's home at Fair Lane. Ford had been thinking about the development of this site for at least two years. He was attracted by its great size, which made expansive single-story construction feasible, and he also saw another advantage. He had observed that smooth, rapid internal operations meant little unless the materials could be brought to the plant and the product taken away with the same ease. For that the Rouge site was ideal; it was served by major rail lines, including a direct connection to Highland Park, and also by the river itself, which linked Rouge to the vital Great Lakes ports. Development of the Rouge site for Eagle boat production seemed especially logical because the shallow-draft boat could be launched directly into the river. A portion of the river was widened and dredged, and the surrounding swampy areas were filled. Subordinate docks, sheds, and launching slips were laid out clustered around the actual manufacturing building.[6]

The Eagle Plant proper, "B" Building as it is known in Ford terminology, consisted of five immense aisles, each 51 feet wide and 1,700 feet long (fig. 29). This enormous volume exceeded by far that of any single area Kahn had designed to that date. The great building is impressive even today, in spite of the fact that it sits among the whole panoply of huge structures comprising the Ford Rouge complex. Aisles B and D (see plan, fig. 30) carried continuous railroad tracks for transport of parts and materials. Aisles A, C, and E were for the boats, which moved from operation to operation until the hull, complete except for power plant, arrived at the south end. There it exited through a 40-foot-high rolling steel door and was conducted by a transfer table to the launching slip 600 feet to the west. All five aisles had a clear height of 30 feet 8 inches except the south 400 feet of aisles A, C, and E, which handled the boat in its nearly completed state and therefore had a clear height of 50 feet 9 inches. All aisles had either monitor or clerestory lighting through operable steel sash. Steel trusses with doubly tapered top chords carried roof loads (figs. 31, 33); a simple superstructure projected upward in monitor-lighted bays. Wind loads were resisted by side walls and by rigid connections between columns and trusses. Roofing was of cement tiles. Running continuously on either long side of the building were low aisles, 26

Figure 29
Ford Motor Company Eagle Plant
on the Rouge River, Detroit, 1917.
(Photograph taken sometime in the
1930s, showing fenestration as
remodeled.) The boat slip for
launching the Eagle submarine
chaser lies just lower left. After the
war the Eagle Plant, as "B" Building
or Shipping Plant, would serve as the
nucleus for the immense Rouge
complex. The Glass Plant of 1922 is
at the extreme left, also shown in its
remodeled state. (See also figure 39.
Photograph courtesy of Albert Kahn
Associates.)

Figure 30
Ford Eagle Plant; plan. (Photograph
by Graydon Miller, courtesy of
Albert Kahn Associates.)

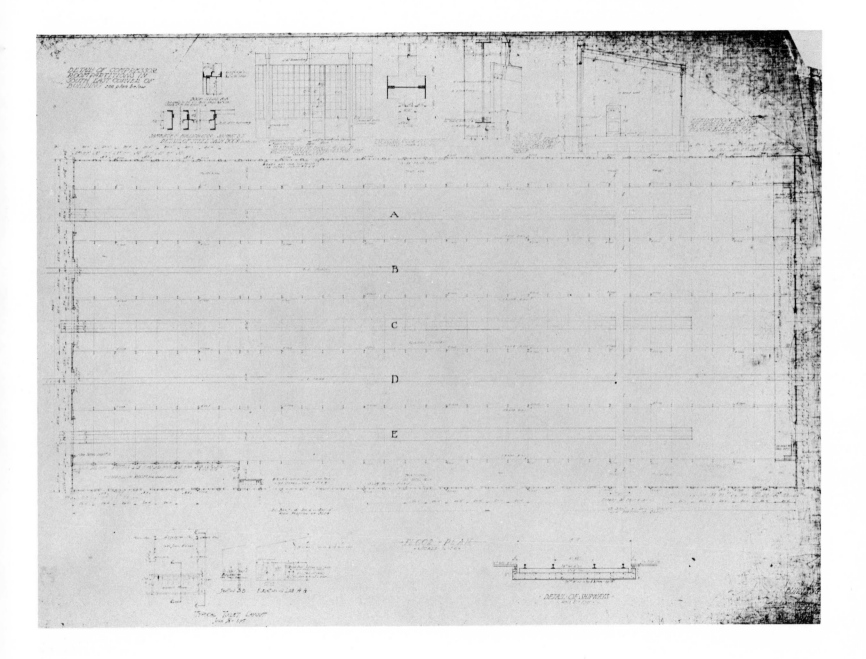

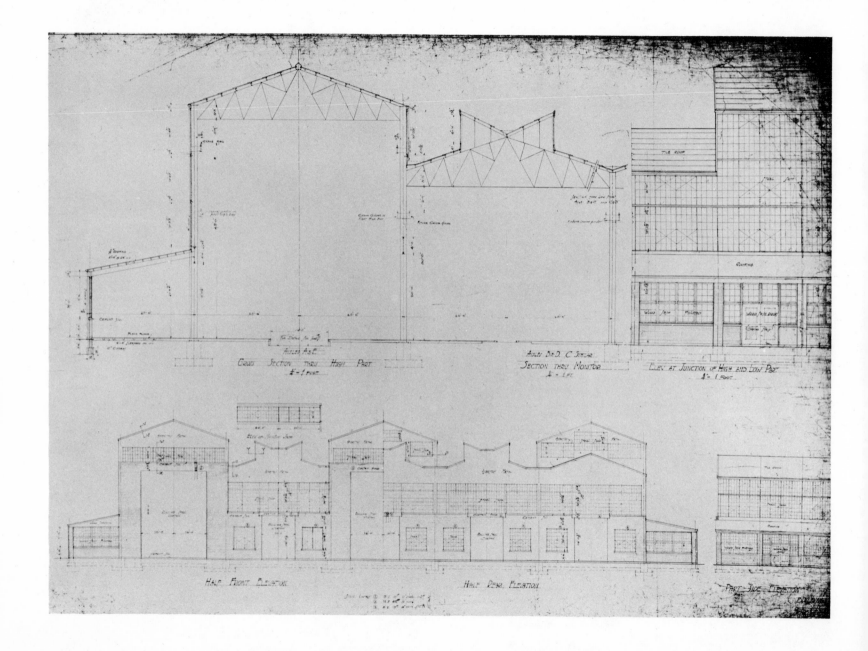

Figure 32
Ford Eagle Plant; exterior in 1918.
(Photograph courtesy of Ford
Archives, Henry Ford Museum.)

Figure 31
Ford Eagle Plant; sections.
(Photograph by Graydon Miller,
courtesy of Albert Kahn Associates.)

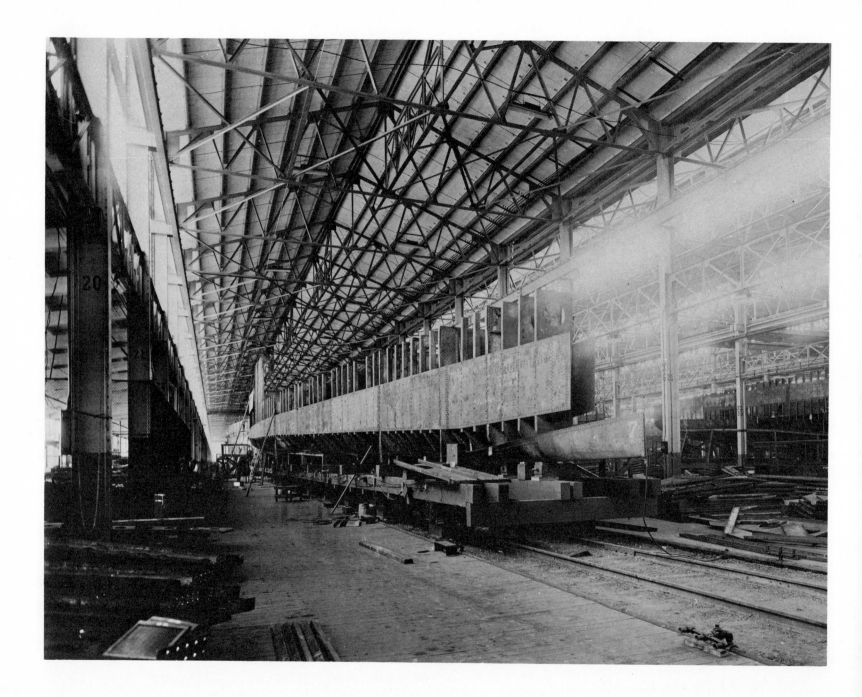

feet wide, housing subsidiary functions including toilets. These aisles were wood framed, wood sheathed in their upper portions, and lighted by windows with wood sash, so they could be easily taken down for later expansion. Brick was used for the lower walls of the plant; high areas were clad in asbestos metal (fig. 32).

The drawings are dated February 11, 1918, less than four weeks after Ford was directed to proceed. The plant was complete within fourteen weeks of the issuance of the drawings. This schedule was four times as rapid as that of the Highland Park Plant and twice as fast as Pierce, and this work was accomplished in spite of the great size of the building. The saving in time was, no doubt, largely due to the steel construction, which eliminated the time-consuming erection of formwork. The *Ford Man* for May 18 summarized the operation:

> As soon as the foundations are ready the superstructure of steel and concrete and glass shoots up; floors are laid while the roof is going on and the glass going in the windows; as the floor progresses machinery is installed; so that when the last arching rafter is in place, the roofer is at hand and when the last shingle is laid all floors, runways, assembly conveyors, machinery, lights, every essential is in place and the big plant is at once at work.[7]

The Eagle Plant is significant for four reasons: it enclosed an immense and complex manufacturing operation within a simple, direct, and economical plan configuration; it marked a major manufacturer's commitment to one-story construction; it was therefore framed in steel, marking the turning of industrial architecture toward light, steel-framed, thinly clad enclosures; and finally, as a result of its steel structure, it was built with remarkable speed. (By August of 1919 intermediate stories were constructed in several areas of the building to convert it for production of Model T bodies and Fordson tractors, but this alteration should not be confused with the intentional multistory scheme at Highland Park. At Rouge it was done to take advantage of a building that had originally been built high enough to handle boat hulls.)[8]

Figure 33
Ford Eagle Plant; interior in 1918.
(Photograph courtesy of Ford
Archives, Henry Ford Museum.)

In 1919 and 1921, despite the continuing pressure of a number of large commissions, Kahn found time for brief trips to Europe. By 1923 this was no longer possible. Ernestine and their daughter Lydia had gone, but he could not find time to break away. The depression of 1920–1921 was over, and his office staff had grown to 200. His brother Moritz (1881–1939), who had been with Julius's firm from 1906 to 1923, joined Albert as an associate in 1923. The Paige Motor Company was a new client, and other things were pending, but as Albert explained in a letter to Ernestine on April 9,

We are continuing to take in new work, largely from Ford. They never before did quite as much and their plans seem without limit. Whether we can hold them is of course always a question. We'll try our darnedest. I'm really glad I had the courage to stay home, though Goodness Knows I wanted to run over to meet you. But so many things have needed my attention this spring—for this is an abnormal year—that I would never have forgiven myself, had I not been on the job.

Ford was in the process of a national decentralization of its manufacturing to reduce shipping costs for the still tremendously popular Model T, and Kahn was designing the plants. They were already under construction in seven major cities; within the next five years twenty-eight more would be built. (Units at Chicago and Minneapolis were of 700,000 square feet each.) The cost of the entire decentralization program was well over $150 million. And eclipsing all this other activity, Rouge was being expanded in all directions to replace Highland Park as the nucleus of the Ford empire. These were the plans without limit to which Kahn was referring.

Henry Ford's urge toward independence is well known. As of 1919 he had bought out all other stockholders to become sole owner of the company. It was then his intention to be independent of suppliers and subcontractors as well. This intention found expression in the Rouge program, which was developed to provide manufacturing units for as many constituent parts of the Model T as possible. Ford already had his own glass made at Highland Park; at Rouge he wanted a plant capable of making 12 million square feet of polished plate glass a year for the Model T windows. The resultant Rouge Glass Plant of 1922 (fig. 34) became the prototype of

Ford buildings of the twenties. Like the Pierce plant, this is a building of the greatest significance both in terms of Kahn's career and in the larger history of industrial architecture. Ford owned glass sand deposits at Carlton, Michigan, which were directly connected by rail line to the sidings at Rouge.

The "batch" is melted in huge furnaces, each with a capacity of 408 tons of molten glass. About 35 tons a day is the amount melted. The temperature maintained is a melting heat of 2500 degrees Fahrenheit and a refining heat of 2300 degrees. The furnaces are charged every 15 minutes with sand, soda ash and other chemicals. The glass flows out in a continuous stream on to a slowly revolving iron drum, and passes under a roller which determines the thickness, and rolls it into a sheet. From the drum it enters the lehr, moving at the rate of 30 to 34 inches a minute. The lehr is 442 feet long and anneals the glass under gradually diminishing heat.

At the end of the lehr the glass is cut into 113-inch lengths . . . and passed on conveyor tables under a series of grinding and polishing machines. Sand mixed with water flows through a hole in the center of the cast iron grinding disc and works its way out to the edge. Finer and finer sand is used as the glass moves on its way, each grinder taking a "cut". . . . The glass then goes to the polishing discs which are felt-covered and use a mixture of iron rouge and water. At the end of the line the glass is turned over and proceeds back up the other grinding and polishing line, emerging completely ground and polished on both sides and a quarter of an inch thinner.[9]

This process organization would have been determined by Ford. At this time and hereafter the policy of the Kahn office was that the manufacturer would handle the process organization since he was most capable of doing so. Moritz Kahn said of the matter, "an architect who specializes in the design of industrial buildings is not expected to be an expert in process layout. The works manager is best capable of preparing his own process diagram. Being in possession of such a diagram, the architect should confine his efforts to building around that layout a factory which is best suited to the scheme of operation."[10] The task of the Kahn office was to devise the appropriate physical enclosure for this process.

The Glass Plant design was completed and plans issued on October 9, 1922. The processing lines were laid out running north-south, parallel to the lines of the Eagle Plant. The four great furnaces are ranged across the south end (see plan, fig. 35). Storage and mixing bins are immediately west of the furnaces. Raw materials are brought to these bins by the rail spur running inside the entire west wall. Each furnace feeds three process lines to its north: a lehr, a grinding line, and a polishing line. A large storage space lies to the north of the lines. A 40-foot-wide balcony for toilets, lockers, and supervision crosses the building at about the midpoint. All functions are contained within a simple 280-foot by 750-foot rectangular plan except that a 20-foot by 100-foot projection is necessary at the southeast corner in order to enclose the east furnace.

The major part of the building, that is, the area enclosing the process lines, is covered by a roof of alternating large and small monitors (see fig. 35). Each large monitor is located to include a lehr under each of its edges. Thus the highest ceiling and the greatest opportunity for ventilation in this area occur over the lehrs, where the intense heat of annealing must rise and escape (see section, figs. 36 and 37). The grinding and polishing lines receive light and a lesser degree of ventilation either directly through the small monitors or indirectly, across the lehr, from the high monitors. This monitor system is interrupted only by the balcony, whose higher roof carries two runs of small monitors in an east-west direction. The westernmost 40 feet of the building, over the rail spur, has a roof that is at the same height as that above the balcony and is provided with similar monitors. Continuous craneways serve this area and all grinding and polishing lines.

The highest monitored roof occurs over the furnaces, where temperatures are greater than anywhere else in the building. The rising heat can escape through continuous expanses of operable sash 25 feet in vertical dimension. Between the west furnace and the rail spur the conveying and batch-mixing equipment is housed in a gable-roofed turret. Wind loads are resisted by X bracing in occasional bays of side walls, the bracing lying inside the plane of the sash. The building is additionally stiffened by X bracing in the plane of the lower chords of the trusses.

It is noteworthy that in the Glass Plant (as in the Packard Forge Shop and the Eagle Plant but not the Machine Shop at Highland Park) no attempt has been made to use glazing to provide only north light; the Glass Plant monitors face four cardinal directions. In plants where north light alone is provided, light distribution is less uniform than with monitors facing two or more

Figure 34
Ford Glass Plant, 1922; exterior.
(Photograph courtesy of Albert Kahn
Associates.)

Figure 35
Ford Glass Plant; plan. (Redrawn
from the original by Mrs. Lois
Wardell.)

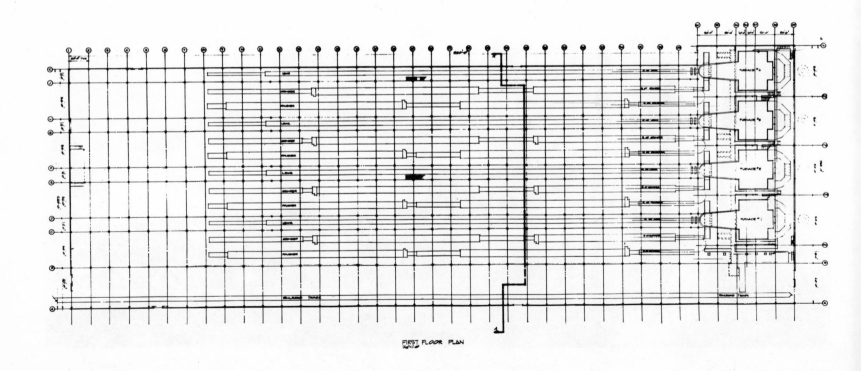

FIRST FLOOR PLAN

Figure 36
Ford Glass Plant; section through
process lines. (Photograph by
Graydon Miller, courtesy of Albert
Kahn Associates.)

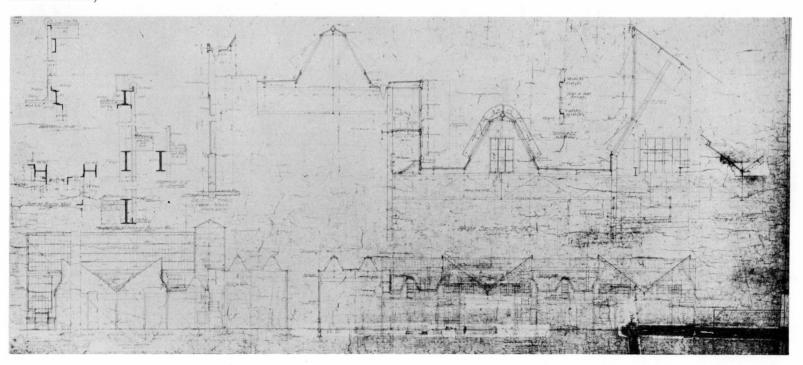

Figure 37
Ford Glass Plant; details of sections.
(Redrawn from the original by Mrs.
Lois Wardell.)

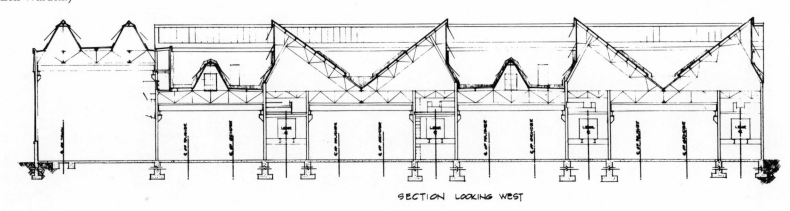

SECTION LOOKING WEST

Figure 38
Ford Glass Plant; details of sections.
(Photograph by Graydon Miller,
courtesy of Albert Kahn Associates.)

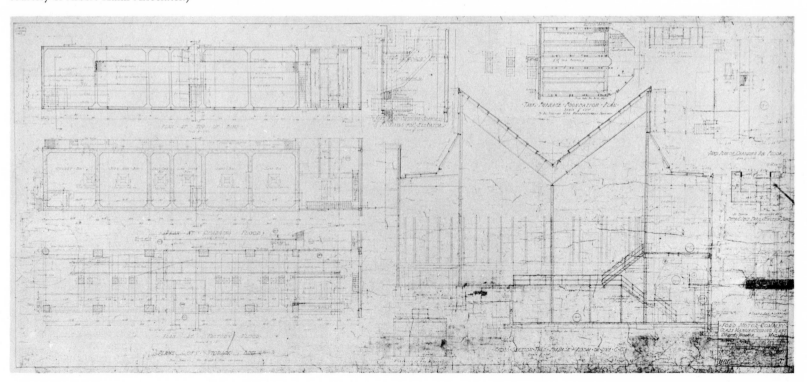

directions. More important, however, where north light alone is provided, the working lines must run at right angles to the glazing, and thus the flexibility of the entire plant is limited. Both Ford and Kahn realized at an early date that the costs of such a limitation exceeded the benefits; thus sawtooth roofs do not appear in Kahn's work after 1920. This is not true, incidentally, of other designers in the industrial field. The Austin Company, for example, perhaps the most famous industrial architectural firm after Kahn's, was using sawtooth systems as late as 1940. So far as is now known, Kahn was the only major figure to dispense with the sawtooth permanently at an early date. He probably did so because he did not concentrate on the question of lighting in isolation but recognized the full range of needs impinging on the building's design.

The parts of the Glass Plant superstructure that carry the smaller monitors are framed by simple trusses (see fig. 37). These trusses are carried on lines of columns, which, angling inward at about sixty degrees as they move upward, also support the upper portions of the sloping trusses belonging to the large monitors. At their lower ends these sloping trusses meet to form the valley of the large monitor; there they can rest on another horizontal truss that spans across the grinding and polishing lines to columns located between these lines and the lehr; these latter columns also carry the craneways. Over the furnaces, sloping trusses also follow the monitor profile, but since no process line occurs under the valley, columns placed there carry directly the lower ends of the trusses (see fig. 38). The structure seems complex, as indeed it is, but what should be noted is the high degree of integration among the processes, the equipment necessary to serve them, the needs of light and ventilation, and the building's structure and form. The more one studies this integrated quality, the more sophisticated and fascinating it appears.

Cladding materials are used in horizontal stratified zones (fig. 34). Brick masonry forms the base whose upper limit varies in height but is never more than 14 feet above grade. Above this the wall materials are exclusively steel and glass—either "Hyrib" corrugated steel sheathing or steel sash. These materials are used in large simple sweeps of coverage. Furthermore, they lie slightly outside the line of structural columns and the refore pass by the columns without abutting them. The handling of wall materials, therefore, allows a small number of typical connection techniques to apply throughout. The plan configuration, too, is simple. These features make for significant economies in a number of ways, since they mean faster production of drawings, quicker and more reliable bidding, easier setting out of the work on the site, and simpler ordering and scheduling. As a result the building tends to be intrinsically inexpensive, but more importantly the plant is in production sooner, and, as the Pierce Company had stated as early as 1906, this is the crucial element in the economic equation.

The design of this building is remarkable. At the time, most manufacturers were still erecting multistory, reinforced-concrete, wall-window structures. As late as 1933, in a rare coverage of industrial architecture the *Journal of the Royal Institute of British Architects*[11] illustrated an article with buildings of that type. In 1927, five years after the Glass Plant, the presumably aware Italian Fiat firm hired the architect Giaccomo Matté-Trucco to design a completely new plant. The scheme that Matté-Trucco evolved was a multistory complex in which raw materials started at the ground floor and moved upward through the building to emerge at roof level as the completed car, which was then driven around the roof test track and down a helix to the ground. Reyner Banham has called this factory "the most nearly Futurist building ever built."[12] In fact, in its structure and materials, even in its spans, floor heights, facades, and glazing details, the Fiat factory is a near-replica of Ford Highland Park. Its planning is simply the Highland Park scheme turned upside-down (and thereby deprived of the gravity-feed principle). But in terms of Kahn's career Highland Park is of an entirely different era from the Glass Plant.

Other progressive industrial architects of the time were dealing with the sawtooth roof in concrete or steel. The patented Ballinger Super-Span system, by the Ballinger Company, Architects, is representative of some of the most advanced thinking in industrial architecture apart from Kahn's own efforts. The glazed face of the sawtooth was structured as a truss. Another truss ran at right angles with its lower and upper chords in the planes of the valleys and peaks, respectively, of the sawteeth. Members in the planes of the sloping glazing and the sloping roof

served as the diagonals of this second truss. Spans of up to 100 feet were possible with economy. The Super-Span system was a clever, adaptable solution and was used quite frequently during the twenties. In the design of the Glass Plant, however, Kahn had discarded glazing to a single orientation as overly limiting to arrangements of process lines and manufacture, and in his approach to structure he attempted to evolve, not a typical, but a very specific response to the processes to be housed. Though the Kahn office could reduce some aspects of factory design to formula, it was the approach and typical criteria that were standardized, not the physical solution.

Two points about the Glass Plant, then, especially bear noting. The first is that the steel structural cage was studiously worked out to accommodate precisely the various needs of the manufacturing operation. Second, the materials to sheathe this cage were handled in broad, uninterrupted planar sweeps to simplify the joining conditions, resulting in a simple and economical prismatic envelope. If one were forced to name a single factory that carried industrial architecture forward more than any other, this would most likely be it. Whether or not the Glass Plant is revolutionary is perhaps a moot point; probably it has as much right to the term as any other building of the twentieth century.

Understandably, subsequent work at Rouge evolved from this example. Between 1922 and 1926 Kahn designed and saw constructed at Rouge the Coke Ovens and By-products Plant (1922), the Job Foundry (1923), the Cement Plant (1923), the Open Hearth Building (1925), the Motor Assembly Building (1924–1925), the Pressed Steel Building (1925), the Spring and Upset Building (1925), and a number of smaller structures and additions (see fig. 39). Of these the first three were sufficiently specialized in nature that they followed the tradition of buildings for their particular use; the remainder developed from the principles of the Glass Plant design.

The Open Hearth Building of 1925 is a good example of the latter. In keeping with his goal of self-sufficiency for Rouge, Ford wanted this structure in order to produce the company's own steel. He had in mind a revolutionary process of continuous production of the steel, which involved keeping a reservoir of molten metal constantly in the furnaces to be drawn off as needed (and

Figure 39
Ford Rouge River complex in 1938. The Eagle Plant is at extreme left center, the Glass Plant just to the right of it. The Pressed Steel and Spring and Upset buildings are in foreground; immediately beyond is the Rolling Mill, and beyond at right center the Open Hearth Building. The Power House and Coke Ovens are upper left of center. The river itself appears at upper right with its dredged turning basin and loading slips. Rail service is available on all sides. Most of the buildings shown except the Eagle Plant are from the twenties; all those named are by Kahn. (Photograph courtesy of Albert Kahn Associates.)

simultaneously replenished) for pigging and immediate transfer to the forging presses. But this was one of Ford's less successful ideas, and in the end he had to revert to the slower traditional methods.[13]

The site was near the river, at the south end of the slip. This land was poor for building. It was swampy, with bedrock 100 feet down, so that pile foundations were necessary. Nevertheless, not one, but four identical structures were projected—one to the east and two to the west of the unit actually built. Plans for this unit were issued February 21, 1925; the plant was first put in operation on June 21, 1926.

In plan the building is the familiar economical rectangle, 240 by 1,066 feet. Provision was made for ten furnaces located on a common centerline 67 feet inside the east wall. Of these only the central four were provided originally. The furnaces rest on grade, but to afford accessibility at an upper level as well, a steel-framed mezzanine with a brick floor extends over approximately the western two-thirds of the building (see plans, figs. 41 and 42, and section, fig. 43). This mezzanine serves to bring raw materials to the charging level of the furnaces. Since the materials are unusually heavy and difficult to handle, they are carried on cars running on a system of railroad tracks, which bring the various materials to the final charging track running along the west face of the furnaces. At the lower or pouring level, tracks carry receiving vat cars directly under the furnace ladles where the molten steel is drawn off.

As in the Glass Plant the large monitor with 20-foot-high faces of glass is centered over the row of furnaces, providing the maximum of light and, above all, ventilation to this area. Wind loads are countered by X bracing in side walls and roofs.

Unlike the Glass Plant, however, in the Open Hearth Building the process is really related to the furnace operation alone; the rest is transportation of raw and processed material, weighing, mixing, supervision, personnel services, and so forth. Thus the demands made by the annealing and grinding lines of the Glass Plant have no counterpart in the Open Hearth Building, and the structure is consequently much simpler. Horizontal trusses used in simple spans carry

Figure 41
Ford Open Hearth Building; grade-
level plan. (Photograph by Graydon
Miller, courtesy of Albert Kahn
Associates.)

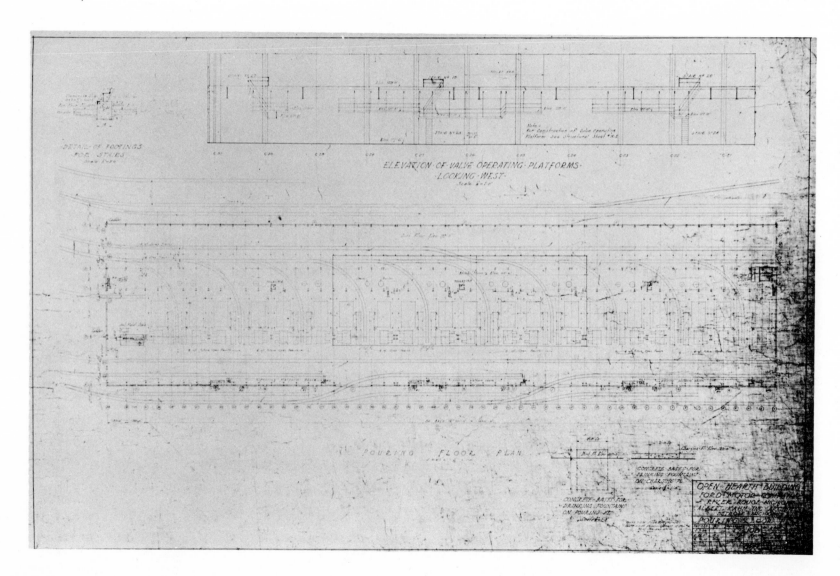

Figure 42
Ford Open Hearth Building;
mezzanine plan. (Photograph by
Graydon Miller, courtesy of Albert
Kahn Associates.)

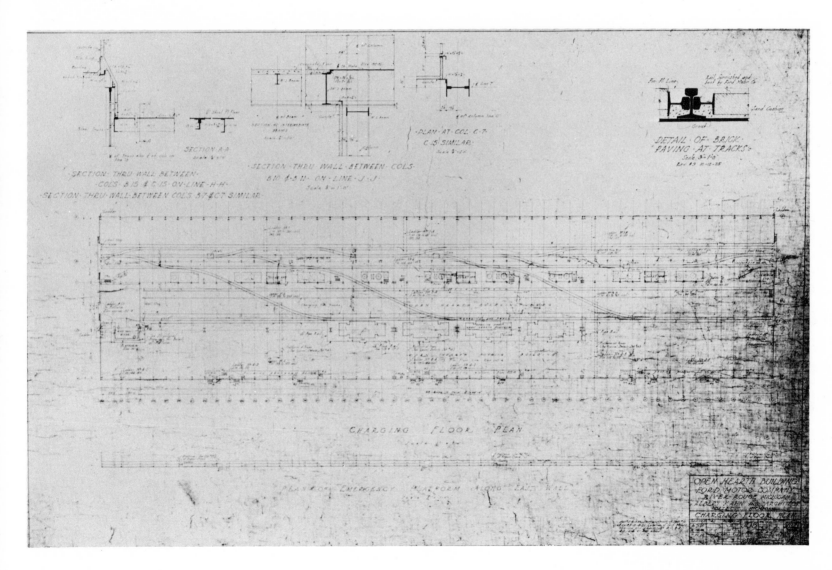

Figure 43
Ford Open Hearth Building;
sections. (Photograph by Graydon
Miller, courtesy of Albert Kahn
Associates.)

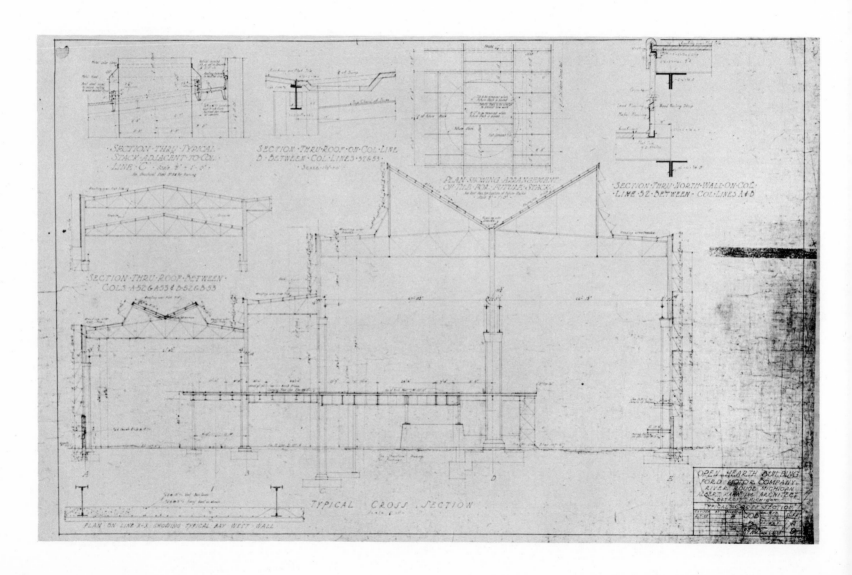

superstructures made up of light steel members that support the monitors (fig. 43). The system over the western portion of the building, particularly, presages Kahn's roof systems of the next decade. The base of the building is clad in brick. Upper portions use large rectilinear expanses of glass and Gunite, a sprayed-on mineral coating usually used in a two-inch thickness (fig. 40).

Of all of Kahn's work at Rouge in the twenties the Motor Assembly Building represents the greatest refinement in treatment of the envelope (see figs. 44 and 45). All wall surfaces on any face are held to a single plane, and fenestration within the plane is even simpler than that of either the Glass Plant or the Open Hearth Building. The roof structure is basically that of the Open Hearth Building, but the overall roof configuration is simpler, resulting in fewer flashing and roofing complexities and fewer atypical structural and joining conditions. The Motor Assembly Building provides a link between Kahn's developments at Rouge and his factories of the following decade.

R. T. Walker is reported to have said of the planning of Rouge as a total complex, "I think the Rouge was pretty much like Topsy, I think that it pretty much just grew." Ford himself commented on the location of a new unit, "Well, push it over plenty far, we don't know what we're going to put around it."[14] But what Rouge did have to assist its growth was, as Ford's comment reveals, an underlying preoccupation with growth itself. Ford's concern for adequate room to enlarge any operation (as illustrated by the three extra projected Open Hearth Buildings) formed in practice a useful planning "policy." One could argue, of course, that all that space between buildings meant just so much more circulation to be provided. In that regard, locating the operations contiguously would have had an advantage, and that kind of planning did govern most of Kahn's work of the next decade (see the Glenn L. Martin Company complex, fig. 79). But on a pragmatic basis Rouge worked well. If Henry Ford had not insisted on producing the Model T after it had become a fossil, Rouge might have worked even better. The rate of growth of the company probably would not have been slowed, and units such as the extra three Open Hearth Buildings might have been built before the depression of 1929, in which case relationships

Figure 44
Ford Rouge River complex in 1938,
looking north; the Eagle Plant is at
center, the Motor Assembly Building
at extreme right center. (Photograph
courtesy of Albert Kahn Associates.)

Figure 45
Ford Motor Assembly Building,
1924–1925; exterior. (Photograph
courtesy of Ford Archives, Henry
Ford Museum.)

among all buildings would have been more nearly contiguous. That was what Ford was providing for; his decisions on other matters simply prevented it from occurring.

The other consideration that was useful in the growth of Rouge was the clarity of the circulation matrix. This is beautifully illustrated in figure 39. All major rail and street lines and the slip itself run north-south, and major process lines in all buildings from the Eagle Plant onward are oriented north-south, providing a basic relationship among all buildings whatever their location. At Highland Park, Ford had also insisted on room for growth, but Highland Park did not by any means have the clear circulation matrix of Rouge. This probably derived from Ford's focus on the process line after 1913. Instinctively he would have seen the plan from that point of view and would have wished to avoid process cross traffic. Henry E. Edmunds, Director of Ford Archives, believes that Kahn also served informally in the planning of Rouge, in addition to his role as architect for individual buildings.[15] Organizational roles at Ford were not often spelled out in detail in the twenties, and it is not only possible but probable that Kahn played an occasional role as de facto planner. The point is raised because of the similarity between the circulation matrix at Rouge and that governing the Pierce layout of 1906. Thus one might wonder about the degree to which the Pierce Plant was seen as a precedent for Kahn's assembly-line design of the twenties, and Ford Rouge work in particular. On this point one can only enumerate the prototypal features of Pierce: a one-story roof-lighted plan of indeterminate horizontal extension, organized on a common module with reference to a clear circulation matrix. It is entirely possible that Kahn perceived the appropriateness of the Pierce scheme to the assembly method, which considerably postdated it; but unless we have some detailed knowledge of conversations between Ford and Kahn at the time (which we don't), the matter can only be conjecture. Probably the best conclusion is that, in talking such things over, the two men served as mutual catalysts for one another's ideas.

Rouge   Rouge was admired by Moholy-Nagy of the Bauhaus, among others, and he included a
photograph of it, without mentioning the architect, in his *Von Material zu Architektur* of 1929.[16] In
Vers une Architecture[17] Le Corbusier also used photographs of American factory buildings, and
Gropius expressed his admiration for "the newest work halls of the North American industrial
trusts [which appealed to him because of] their overwhelming monumental power." None of
these men of the European avant-garde, however, went beyond the inspirational or symbolic
value that could be extracted from the aesthetic aspects of factory design. The sophistication of
design and planning that made Rouge what it was went unprobed. In the United States, Rouge
was published in engineering and industrial journals but did not appear in architectural
publications, conservative or avant-garde, for either aesthetic inspiration or its interest as an
example of more practical aspects of design. Yet as such an example, it was the most important
industrial complex of its time.

Its closest rival was probably the Krupp complex at Essen, but Krupp's methods of
manufacture, and particularly of assembly, did not drive its factory design to such far-reaching
solutions. The Krupp works were vast, even by the time of Highland Park's construction, and
included immense assembly sheds comparable in scale to the Rouge "B" Building built eight
years later. These sheds were roofed over by arched steel beams or trusses carrying glass roofs, so
that the whole effect was similar to many Victorian train sheds or to Behrens's A.E.G. Turbine
Factory of 1908, which was discussed earlier. The great Krupp guns were assembled inside these
sheds but not on assembly lines. Because of their size and weight, they were put together at fixed
stations on the shed floor, and small parts were brought to the assembly stations by cart, large
parts by huge overhead cranes traveling the length of the halls. This method of operation had
implications both for individual buildings and for the overall arrangement of the complex. It
meant that the buildings were more independent entities whose flow patterns were not indissolubly
linked to those of the entire complex, so that buildings could use varying structural modules,
varying orientations, and sawtooth roofs oriented to north light as required. For small-parts

manufacture unrelated to a mechanized assembly line, they could also be several stories in height. In terms of the total complex, relationships among buildings could be looser and more random, and policies of movement and flow were less apparent in the planning, which to some extent simply appears to have followed the medieval street plan of Essen.

Whether such a physical plant was most efficient for the production of heavy armaments is not entirely clear. Like any manufacturer, Krupp would have wanted to keep costs as low as possible, but he was under less pressure to do so than Ford because of the nature of the product. Krupp weaponry was sold, not on the basis of low cost, but on the basis of high destructiveness; if it fulfilled that goal better than its competitors, there was a considerable latitude in pricing. Thus Krupp annals show attention to other aspects of business, stressing in particular technical innovation, salesmanship, and international politics, but there is no recorded indication that Krupp was concerned with architecture as a key to profitable manufacturing operations.[18] Until the time of the plant's destruction in 1943–1945 many of the buildings were multistory, many utilized brick bearing walls with punched windows, and all seem to have been conceived as more or less separate entities. Those that used roof lighting depended on skylights in arched roofs or sawtooth systems glazed to the north. Thus building design at Krupp tended to follow patterns laid down between 1890 and 1910, and relationships among buildings never reached the stage represented by Kahn's Pierce Plant of 1906. By comparison, Rouge as an entity was committed to several objectives that challenged both design and planning. Of particular importance were its commitments to the assembly line and to limitless but efficient expansion, both in the assumed context of economic competition.[19] For reasons already discussed, these objectives led Kahn to the exclusive study of the steel-framed factory building seen as part of a larger matrix. In this study he found innovative integrated solutions to problems of process, light, ventilation, and structure; and he began to develop a simplified—that is, more rapidly and cheaply constructed— envelope. The continued study of this last aspect, the efficient envelope, was the focus of his efforts of the following decade.

We have examined the technical planning advances of Rouge. What of its humanistic contributions? Unfortunately, as at Highland Park, there is little more than conjecture, and for similar reasons. Ventilation in the hot Open Hearth Building and the Glass Plant certainly would have aided human comfort, and all the buildings at Rouge were notable for their excellent lighting, which presumably contributed to a happier working environment. Rouge was also sparklingly clean and constantly painted from end to end. The open hearth operation, for example, which elsewhere was traditionally filthy, was spotless at Rouge; all parts of the building were scrubbed and painted. But at Rouge, far more than at Highland Park, architectural devices were bent toward productivity rather than human contentment. Labor relations deteriorated sharply from the relatively progressive days of 1914–1915 at Highland Park. Allan Nevins, probably the best commentator we have on Ford, says of Rouge, "One would gladly write that its bold planning and fine mechanization, its large, well-lighted, clean and efficiently ventilated structures were matched by a happy spirit among its officials and workers. Unfortunately, the reverse became true."[20] This occurred as a consequence of certain changes in the company itself, all of which tended toward harsher labor policies. Most important were some changes in key labor-related executive personnel. In 1921 Dr. Samuel Marquis, formerly the intelligent leader of sociological benevolence at Ford, resigned, and his resignation marked the beginning of a much tougher period. Charles Sorensen directed most aspects of operation pertaining to working conditions, and he was a driver, who had already done much to obstruct Marquis's work. William C. Klann, an executive in touch with shop conditions, said in the very year of the erection of the Glass Plant, "Ford was one of the worst shops for driving the men."[21] There were reasons for this, chief among them the depression and resultant severe financial difficulties of the company. Nevertheless, in spite of seemingly excellent architectural conditions, it must be said that Rouge was not a happy place to work in the mid-twenties. Architecture can benefit the human condition when it operates in conjunction with equally humanitarian policies and attitudes, but without these its effects are negated.

One other Ford building of the twenties is of interest in terms of Kahn's factory work. This is the Engineering Laboratory at Dearborn, drawings for which are dated September 14, 1922. It is not strictly an industrial building in the sense of the factories, and it was not built on a restricted budget. In fact, it has a dry neoclassic exterior. The interior, however, is notable for its remarkably clean steel and concrete structure and for its sloped monitor faces, which provide a given level of illumination with less glass and less building height and tend also to be self-cleaning (fig. 46). As in the 1914–1915 additions to the Highland Park Plant, hollow columns carry ductwork for air distribution.

Though the work for Ford at Rouge was the nucleus of Kahn's practice in the twenties, it was not by any means his sole effort. The highlights of his nonindustrial work will be discussed in the next chapter. In the industrial field, in addition to Rouge, he was designing the already mentioned thirty-five branch plants for Ford. The earlier of these were multistory buildings of reinforced concrete following the format of the Highland Park work. Plants at Chicago, Louisville, Memphis, and Jacksonville, however, followed the Rouge model of steel-framed, single-story, monitor-lighted construction. When Ford purchased the Lincoln Motor Company of Detroit in 1923, Kahn designed a large steel-framed addition to the plant. And throughout the twenties, no doubt partly because of his association with the vast Ford projects, Kahn gained additional important automotive clients.

Early in the decade he designed reinforced-concrete factories for Studebaker Corporation and Fisher Body Corporation. In 1925 Chrysler Corporation was formed. It bought from Chalmers Motor Company the East Jefferson Avenue plant that Kahn had designed in 1907 and the old Maxwell Motor Company plant in Highland Park. Kahn was commissioned to do extensive steel-framed additions to each of these. In 1928 he designed the Engineering Building for Chrysler Corporation. In the same year Chrysler established Plymouth Motor corporation, and Kahn was immediately commissioned to do the vast and completely new plant at Mt. Elliot Avenue and Lynch Road. This was again a one-story, steel-framed, monitor-lighted factory of extensive scope,

Figure 46
Ford Motor Company Engineering
Laboratory, Dearborn, Michigan,
1922; interior. (Photograph courtesy
of Ford Archives, Henry Ford
Museum.)

smaller by far than the total Rouge complex but larger than any single unit completed at that time.

In 1929 Kahn did his first work for the aircraft industry, a factory for the Glenn L. Martin Company at Middle River, Maryland, fourteen miles north of Baltimore. The monitored roof was similar to that of the Ford Engineering Laboratory (see fig. 79); otherwise, the plant itself was not exceptional. More significant was the fact that this was the first of a series of buildings for Glenn Martin. Martin had been one of the pioneers of aviation. In 1912, as a pilot, he flew the first mail route and a year later was test pilot for the Army in its experiments with aerial bombs. He had been a stunt pilot in early movie days and had appeared with Mary Pickford on one occasion. In 1910 he built his first airplane in an abandoned California church. His natural sense of mechanics and his willingness to combine inventiveness with commercial venture are reminiscent of Henry Ford. Possibly the similarity occurred to Kahn, too; certainly Kahn and Martin developed a similarly close rapport, with the consequence that virtually all building projects for Martin from 1929 through 1942 were done by Kahn. The 1929 unit, then, while not remarkable in itself, was the first of a series of buildings, several of which would be of considerable significance.

Office Structure and Organization

Thus, between the depression of 1921 and the crash of 1929, in addition to numerous smaller industrial projects and a great quantity of nonindustrial work, Kahn's office designed some fifty-odd major factories. By early 1929 the firm was producing one million dollars' worth of construction a week. The total staff had grown to more than 400. Within this huge firm there was no question at any time about the ultimate authority, however. Throughout his career Kahn was a rigorous administrator and an arduous taskmaster; he demanded and got intense and concentrated effort from all employees and associates at all times. Standards were exacting, and discipline was firm. One story that is told by a few old-timers is of a man dismissed for having been caught smoking in the men's room. Though probably apocryphal, the story does convey the flavor of a tightly disciplined organization. Kahn was equally firm about intramural bickering.

He wanted a team, and backbiting was a sure way not to get it. His treatment was effective: anyone complaining about another was immediately brought to Kahn's office, along with the defendant. There the complainant could either state his case or drop the matter forever. Kahn furthermore firmly required the subordination of individual personalities to the team effort. Prima donnas repressed their egos or were dismissed. Allan Nevins has described a similar situation at Ford Motor Company under Henry Ford.

> . . . Ford insisted on having engineers who, while capable of original solutions, were willing to subordinate their ideas to his own penetration and originality. He regarded their designs as raw material for change and adaption. In an era of large industrial enterprise, a group effort under one specially gifted leader is after all the best key for unlocking technological problems.[22]

Whether Kahn drew his operational philosophy from this source or was just responding intuitively to the firm's needs and his own personality we do not know. Possibly it was a little of both. In any case his insistence on smooth team effort under a single guiding hand is clear. Throughout the twenties, and in fact until 1935, Kahn hired no college graduate with an architectural degree, for what he considered an extremely important reason: as he saw it, the graduate architect often tended to place self-expression over team cooperation and so was simply not suitable for the kind of organization Kahn had built. This was of course an extreme policy, and one that probably cost the office the services of a number of talented men. But the urge for self-expression in the graduate architect can be strong, and Kahn's solution, extreme though it was, illustrates his equally strong feeling on the matter. He referred to himself as the quarterback or, more poetically, the conductor of the symphony. There were to be few solo performances; the objective was the direction of many talents toward an end impossible to achieve by any single participant.[23]

A detailed breakdown of the areas of expertise within the firm in the late twenties is not available, but those who were there at the time recall that the office was intensifying its commitment to full representation of all pertinent skills. This is supported by the comments of Moritz Kahn in 1929:

It would be expecting too much of any designer to be master of all the principles that enter into the design of industrial buildings, and therefore the architect who wishes to specialize in this field of work is well advised in surrounding himself with a staff of assistants, each of whom will be especially qualified in his particular sphere.[24]

Is there a connection between Henry Ford's concern for a self-sufficient industrial complex at Rouge and Albert Kahn's increasingly self-contained architectural office? One wonders if the two men ever talked it over.

The Russian Venture

The economic problems following the autumn of 1929 are too familiar to need retelling; their effect on the number of architectural commissions available was similar to their effect on other aspects of the economy. Industrial architecture was particularly affected. As automobile production fell from its high in 1929 to its low in 1932, no one was interested in building new factories. Thus Kahn's industrial practice would have languished if his reputation had not brought to him in April of 1929 an amazing commission from the Soviet Union. This was a time which the USSR was doing a considerable bit of international recruiting in all fields. Among architects, for example, Frank Lloyd Wright and the Welshman Clough Williams-Ellis toured Russia and were offered work. For an industrial architect, however, the Russians wanted Kahn. A $40 million tractor plant at Chelyabinsk was specifically commissioned by the Amtorg Trading Corporation, the Russian international commerce liaison, with the hint that this might lead to an additional $2 billion worth of less clearly defined projects.

Nevertheless, the commission was not easy to accept, particularly since when it was offered the crash was six months away and work in the United States was still available in abundance. Kahn detailed his reservations:

... I was somewhat hesitant about accepting such a task. First, I knew little or nothing about the Russian government, and the people behind it. Second, the United States had refused to recognize that government. Third, there was a feeling against Communists among the people with whom I had to do business. Fourth, the enemies of my people echoed what the Nazis were saying and accused the Jews of fostering Communism. I wondered what would be said if I took the job. And yet the challenge fascinated me. . . . I believed that the Russian people—regardless of their form of government—were entitled to help after all their generations of suffering under the czars. The more I thought about it the more I became convinced it was the right thing to do.[25]

At first the work was done in the Detroit office, but Moritz was soon sent to Moscow with a staff of twenty-five to open a branch office. In part this move represented a more expedient means for carrying out a very large volume of work, but it also suited the purposes of the Soviet Union, for the objective was only partly the design of the plants themselves. Organizational and design skills, techniques, and experience were also to be passed on to the Russian architectural and engineering professions. Days were given over to an on-the-job training program in actual factory design. In the evening, classes were given by the Kahn staff. By the time the branch office was dissolved and the staff sent home in March 1932, 521 plants large and small had been designed, and over 4,000 Russian personnel had participated in the training program. A telegram sent to Mrs. Kahn by V. A. Vesnin at the time of Kahn's death in 1942 stated that " . . . Mr. Albert Kahn . . . helped us to assimilate the American experience in the sphere of the building industry."[26]

Of the many Russian plants there is only a small amount of information available. The tractor plant at Chelyabinsk was a mammoth affair of 100-foot spans and 40-foot roof heights. The other factories of which we know anything at all derive from the Ford Rouge work; the plants at both Kuznetsk and Stalingrad were so similar to Rouge that they could easily be mistaken for it. The similarity was not happenstance. Kahn was more involved with Ford work than any other in the twenties, so that any subsequent work would logically build on that at Rouge, but furthermore in May of 1929 the Ford Motor Company had also been recruited by Amtorg following a series of interviews and overtures dating back to 1926. Ford was to provide products, services, and training, and a large Ford staff was actually stationed in Russia until 1933, transferring techniques, methods, experience, and actual verbatim designs to the Russians. The Russians had "full right to make, sell, and use Ford units throughout the USSR, to make and use Ford machinery and other equipment, and to use all Ford inventions or technical advances patented or unpatented."[27]

This is about all we know of the great volume of work done in the USSR. The contribution of these plants to the development of Kahn's factory vocabulary, however, was hindered in one respect by the fact that, according to Kahn's account, they were heavily overdesigned and thus not efficient in use of materials, at least not by the usual standards. Moritz guessed that the overdesign was demanded because of the expectation that sooner or later the plants would probably be involved in, and would be targets of, war. Those at Stalingrad, of course, eventually were put to the acid test and apparently stood up to it. They produced the equipment that turned the tide of land war in the east in September 1941.

In March 1932 the Russians terminated the relationship. Albert Kahn went to Moscow personally to attempt to negotiate a new contract, but with no success.

I could not meet their terms. I might have if I had been permitted to send an entirely new group of men which of course are easily had today at very low salaries. But they insisted on having the same heads—most of whom cared little about staying at all and certainly not at materially reduced wages. So there was nothing to be done . . . the men left a day or so after I did. . . . Russia is considerably pressed for want of gold. They could pay us any number of rubles but what use could they be? One can't use them outside of Russia and even there they count for but little. One thing I am very glad of is that our men did an excellent job, praised by everyone there and we left with the respect and acclaim of the country. They no doubt had a difficult time but met the problem splendidly. Most of them are taking advantage of their being in Europe and are traveling for a while . . . for traveling costs with tickets bought in rubles in Moscow are nil. . . . There is of course very little doing at home.[28]

Notes

1. The date is not known more exactly. Allan Nevins and Frank Ernest Hill, *Ford, the Times, the Man, and the Company* (New York: Scribners, 1954), merely say "during 1913 and 1914" and "some of them were unquestionably in concept and practice prior to March 1, 1913" (p. 469). The reason for the vague dating is that the process was an accretion of developments and ideas over time. The authors, however, do note a "dramatic" demonstration of the system on the third floor of the Highland Park Plant in the magneto assembly area: "The time was early spring, 1913" (p. 471). The discussion of the process by Nevins and Hill is one of the most thorough available.

2. Quoted in Allan Nevins and Frank Ernest Hill, *Ford, Expansion and Challenge: 1915–1932* (New York: Scribners, 1957), p. 61.

3. Quoted in ibid., p. 256.

4. The time-element difficulty with steel lies in speed of delivery, seldom a problem with either the concrete or its adjunct formwork.

5. W. Hawkins Ferry, *The Buildings of Detroit: A History* (Detroit: Wayne State University Press, 1968), p. 179.

6. See Nevins and Hill, *Ford, Expansion*, pp. 72–76, for a discussion of the production process and Ford administration relative to this project.

7. Quoted in ibid., p. 72.

8. Kahn also served as Architect-in-Chief of the Army Signal Corps during 1917–1918, at half his usual fee for all work designed. "During the World War Mr. Kahn was very prominent in those activities whereby civilians could render valuable aid to the government and in his professional capacity he had charge of some of the most extensive and important building projects made necessary by that conflict. He planned and supervised the construction of the training schools for the United States Air Service at Langley Field, Hampton, Virginia, and Rockwell Field, San Diego, California. These projects, with the hangars and various other buildings, were immense undertakings. . . ." (Clarence M. Burton, *History of Detroit*, Detroit-Chicago: S. J. Clarke Publishing Co., 1922).

9. *The Ford Industries*, n.a. (Detroit: The Ford Motor Company, 1924), p. 60.

10. *Architectural Forum* 51, No. 3 (September 1929): 272.

11. Vol. 40, No. 8 (February 1933): 301–307.

12. Reyner Banham, *Theory and Design in the First Machine Age* (London: Architectural Press, 1960), p. 193.

13. See Nevins and Hill, *Ford, Expansion*, pp. 289–292.

14. Ibid., pp. 207, 211.

15. Letter to the author, January 7, 1970.

16. Laszlo Moholy-Nagy, *The New Vision*, Daphne M. Hoffman, trans. (New York: George Wittenborn, 1946), p. 64. I am grateful to Dr. Reyner Banham for calling the photograph to my attention.

17. Quoted in Banham, *Theory and Design*, p. 80.

18. The most complete account of Krupp is William Manchester, *The Arms of Krupp 1587–1968* (Boston: Little, Brown, 1968).

19. It would be interesting to be able to record something comparative about the impact of the two different approaches. But this is difficult because the different kinds of products mean different criteria are brought to bear. In only one instance do the two firms find a more or less common product denominator, but even there we have no real comparison to draw. For whereas during Kahn's lifetime Krupp produced weaponry almost exclusively, in the same period the only weapon produced by Ford was the Eagle boat. Few of these saw service before the armistice, and their impact was negligible.

20. Nevins and Hill, *Ford, Expansion*, p. 295.

21. Ibid., p. 354.

22. Ibid., p. 440.

23. Sol King, FAIA, currently President and Director of Architecture, Albert Kahn Associates, Inc., Architects and Engineers, related this information in a number of conversations in the summers of 1966 and 1967. In 1935 Mr. King was the first college graduate with an architectural degree hired by the firm in fifteen years.

24. *Architectural Forum* 51, No. 3 (September 1929): 272.

25. Quoted in Malcolm W. Bingay, *Detroit Is My Own Home Town* (New York: Bobbs-Merrill, 1946), p. 308.

26. This telegram is dated December 16, 1942 (copy held by Mrs. Malbin). "Soviet engineers builders architects send you their sincere sympathy in connection with the death of your husband Mr. Albert Kahn who rendered us great service in designing a number of large plants and helped us to assimilate the American experience in the sphere of building industry. Soviet engineers and architects will always warmly remember the name of the talented engineer and architect Albert Kahn." Signed V. A. Vesnin, Architect Academician.

27. Nevins and Hill, *Ford, Expansion*, p. 677; pp. 673–678 deal with Ford work in Russia in detail.

28. From letters to Ernestine, March 29, 1932, from Berlin; and to Rosalie, April 14, 1932, from Hamburg-Amerika Line at sea.

6

NONINDUSTRIAL WORK, 1916–1932

The General Motors Building

William C. Durant, founder of General Motors Corporation and president from 1908 to 1910 and again from 1916 to 1920, was a man of grand schemes, and the Durant building was one of them. Probably he gave the commission to Kahn in 1917, since the drawings are dated August 2, 1919. The very magnitude of the building, 1,320,000 square feet of floor area, marks it as Durant's brainchild. It is by far the largest of Kahn's commissions to that date, industrial or otherwise, and it indicates both his increasing facility with large commissions and the growing respect he commanded among automobile manufacturers. The name was changed to the General Motors Building when Durant and General Motors parted company in 1920.[1] Construction was completed in 1921.

The site is a few blocks north of the Art Institute and the Public Library, well outside the major business and financial center of Detroit. A complete block was available at the southeast corner of Second Avenue and Grand Boulevard, one block west from Woodward Avenue. The major portion of the 15-story building, independent of the research laboratory, is disposed in a series of eight wings projecting from the central spine (figs. 47 and 48). This scheme was common at the time for apartment buildings, hotels, and hospitals but was rare in office structures; the usual choices were towers, as, for example, Cass Gilbert's Woolworth Building in New York, completed a few years earlier, or, for lower buildings, a peripheral organization around a central court. One significant exception, certainly known to Kahn, was D. H. Burnham's Dime Bank Building of 1913 in downtown Detroit. In that 23-story design two projecting wings were used with a deep, wide space between them, opening to the street. The advantages of such a scheme are that offices have a street outlook and the street itself benefits from more openness. These advantages obviously appealed to Kahn, and the General Motors Building is successful on both counts.

The court voids are filled in at the lower arcade level and are detailed in an Ionic order. This motif is particularly effective at the Grand Boulevard entrance (fig. 49). At this same level the portions of the building that carry floors have Corinthian piers (fig. 50). The floor immediately above these piers is included under a molding and is surmounted by ten floors of uniform and

austere fenestration, above which one floor is delineated by moldings. Two floors carried within a Corinthian order top the building. All areas in which classical detail is used, however, are restrained and subordinated to the overall massing. This massing treatment, crisp and powerful, is the building's strongest quality. Quite aside from the practical advantages already noted, the General Motors Building is a handsome piece of urban sculpture.

The University of Michigan: Clements Library

The William L. Clements Memorial Library for the University of Michigan campus was done immediately after the General Motors Building (the drawings are dated December 14, 1921), and it shares with General Motors the classical arcade motif. The Clements design may have been patterned after Vignola's casino for the Villa Farnese at Caprarola, Italy, which Kahn may have seen in 1919; but this classical influence may also have occurred indirectly through McKim, Mead and White's similar Butler Art Institute of 1917 for Youngstown, Ohio, which Kahn would have known about since his brother Julius was living in Youngstown at the time. In any case Clements represents the closest approach in Kahn's work to the sophisticated elegance of McKim, and it is a close approach indeed (fig. 51).[2] On the exterior the columns are Corinthian, as opposed to the sturdy Ionic of the General Motors Building; they are a perfect choice for this smaller structure, which has an almost Brunelleschian quality in the crisp delicacy of its treatment. This is a bright gem on the Michigan campus. Kahn sensed its fineness and was proud of it; he stated on several occasions that of all the buildings he had done this was his favorite.

Clements was followed in 1922–1923 by the Angell Hall classroom building for the University's College of Literature, Science and Arts (fig. 52), noted for its Lincoln Memorial-like entry, handsomely detailed lobby, and extensive wings of workable loft classroom spaces to the north and south.[3] In addition to this work for the University of Michigan there were a number of large nonindustrial commissions in Detroit. Prominent among these were the Police Headquarters of 1921, a building rather similar to the Detroit Athletic Club, and the 24-story National Bank Building on Woodward Avenue in the heart of downtown Detroit.

Figure 47
The General Motors Building, Detroit, 1917–1921; exterior from the northeast. West Grand Boulevard is in the right foreground; Second Avenue intersects at extreme right. The site of the future Fisher Building is just out of the picture to the right. (Photograph courtesy of Albert Kahn Associates.)

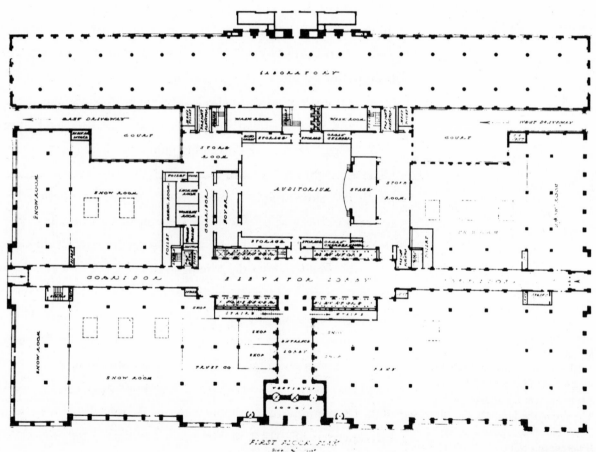

FIRST FLOOR PLAN

GENERAL MOTORS BUILDING
DETROIT MICH.
ALBERT KAHN ARCHITECT

Figure 48
The General Motors Building;
typical floor plans. (Photograph by
Graydon Miller, courtesy of *American
Architect and Building News.*)

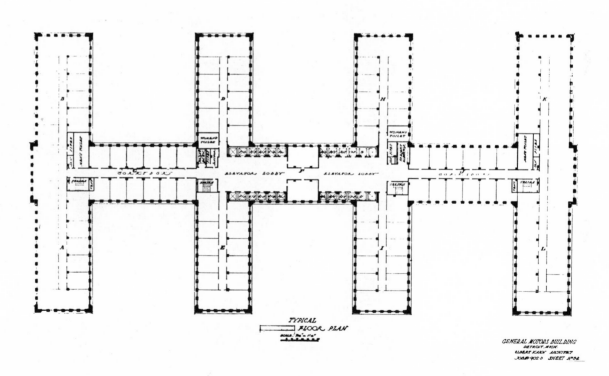

Figure 49
The General Motors Building;
entrance from West Grand
Boulevard. (Photograph by John
Wallace Gillies, courtesy of Albert
Kahn Associates.)

Figure 50
The General Motors Building; street-level arcade. (Photograph courtesy of Albert Kahn Associates.)

Figure 51
The William L. Clements Library,
University of Michigan, Ann Arbor,
1920–1921; exterior from the Law
Quadrangle. (Photograph by
Hedrich-Blessing, courtesy of Albert
Kahn Associates.)

Figure 52
Angell Hall, University of Michigan,
Ann Arbor, 1922–1923; State Street
facade. (Photograph by Hedrich-
Blessing, courtesy of Albert Kahn
Associates.)

Kahn traveled to Europe again in 1919 and 1921. During the two trips he did little sketching, recording his impressions in photographs. The photographs are undated, so their assignment to one trip or the other is conjectural. Two different formats appear, however. To one format belongs a building unidentified and labeled only "Rome," but it is in fact Vignola's casino, which may have influenced the Clements design of 1920.[4] All photographs within its group, therefore, are probably from 1919. Many are of anonymous buildings, and they relate more to the sketches of 1891 than to those of 1912 and, with the exception of the Clements-like building and a few others, far more to Kahn's factories than to his nonindustrial commissions. The rural building complex shown (fig. 53) is typical. Volumes are low, horizontally extended, with parallel, repetitive, stretched-out roofs of identical pitch. Walls and fenestration are direct and simple; in the wing to the left the fenestration is aligned horizontally. While such a building does not relate at all to a work like Clements, it does have similarities to Kahn's factory work (see, for example, figs. 60 and 65). It is unlikely, of course, that Kahn's work would have been influenced by such examples; what does seem clear is that his sensitivities were attuned to these simpler, nonmonumental forms as analogous to his own work. Apparently from the same trip is the magnificent photograph of the staired passageway built through the opening in the massive rubble wall (fig. 54).

The group of photographs presumed to date from 1921 consists of thirty-two large mounted matte prints. Many are of the landscape at Cap Martin, showing the gnarled trees along the rocky coast. Most buildings photographed are again anonymous. In Paris Kahn photographed only the building shown in figure 55. Similar works were selected in Italy at Cremona, Lugano, and Piacenza. There are many photographs of stairways through arched openings, much like that shown in figure 54. There are seven large mounted prints of St. Ambrogio at Milan, the only well-known building selected. St. Ambrogio was then thought to contain the first ribbed groin vaults in Europe and was famous also as an example of Lombard brickmasonry—those were the attributes that would have attracted the scholar or historian at that time. But Kahn was attracted by the play of void against mass as well as the texture and strength of the structural

Figure 53
Rural buildings in Europe, place and
date unknown; a photograph from
Kahn's trip of 1919. Compare with
figures 60 and 65. (Photograph
copied by Joseph Klima, courtesy of
Mrs. Barnett Malbin.)

Figure 54
Europe, place and date unknown; a
photograph from the trip of 1919.
(Photograph copied by Joseph
Klima, courtesy of Mrs. Barnett
Malbin.)

Figure 55
Paris, an anonymous building of
unknown date; from Kahn's trip of
1921. (Photograph copied by Joseph
Klima, courtesy of Mrs. Barnett
Malbin.)

Figure 56
St. Ambrogio, Milan, eleventh to
twelfth century; atrium; photograph
from Kahn's trip of 1921.
(Photograph copied by Joseph
Klima, courtesy of Mrs. Barnett
Malbin.)

material. All seven of the photographs are similar to the one illustrated (fig. 56); all are taken within the atrium, and there are no interiors and no details of the famous Lombard corbel tables. These photographs suggest the part of Kahn's personality that responded to simple bold events, matters not of style but of expressed constructional drama. This he also revealed at Niagara Falls and in his excitement with industry. In this present instance, operating independently of the vogues and tastes that had influenced his 1912 sketches, he recorded monuments of historical importance in his own terms.

The Edsel Ford Home

In 1927, after designing a multitude of factory buildings for Ford Motor Company at Rouge and elsewhere, Kahn was asked by Edsel Ford to design his home in Grosse Pointe. There could hardly be a sharper contrast between Kahn's work at Rouge and this house. It was based on the architecture of the Cotswold Hills of England, of which both Edsel Ford and his father were especially fond. Kahn had had some experience in Tudoresque domestic design dating back to the Charles Swift house in Grosse Pointe of 1903 and the Chandler Walker house in Windsor, Ontario, of 1905. The Edsel Ford house, however, was to be an altogether more elaborate effort and a good bit more of an archaeological adventure. Slates, wood, and paneling—in some cases actually from medieval buildings—were brought over, as were Cotswold workmen. The house shows thorough attention to historic precedent throughout; the roof, for example, is made up of split stones hung on oak boarding with oak pegs, with the stones graded from large at the eaves to small at the ridge, in the Cotswold manner. So, too, all dormer valleys are "swept," the stones turning the angle between the two roof planes in a more or less gentle curve. But in spite of this intended authenticity, the house is a bit too crisp. It has the quality of metal or marble rather than of soft limestone. And of course no great Cotswold wool merchant ever had a residence approaching the Ford house. Vast, rambling, and luxurious, it is clearly a home built on twentieth-century success. Men capable of building on this scale in the Cotswolds, Sir Baptist Hicks of Chipping Campden, for example, appeared only in Stuart times and built in a more urbane style. Another Grosse Pointe house done by Kahn in 1929 for Alvan McCauley, president of the Packard Motor Car Company, was similar but simpler and less picturesque. Kahn enjoyed these commissions. They represented a more personal expression of confidence on the part of his clients, and they provided a pleasant contrast to his larger and sterner tasks.

The Fisher Building

The most important of Kahn's nonindustrial buildings of the late twenties is unquestionably the Fisher Building in Detroit of 1927–1929. It takes its name from the founding brothers of the Fisher Body Corporation, and in keeping with its related interest, it is located diagonally across West Grand Boulevard from the General Motors Building.

The Fisher brothers intended this building to be *their* monument, and no expense was to be spared; it probably had the fewest budget restrictions of any building Kahn ever designed. But a tight budget was a challenge he enjoyed, and he did not feel at ease in its complete absence. A certain amount of his time on the job was given over to preaching the virtues of economy, apparently without much success, since the building is elaborately and expensively fitted. In the end he preferred his General Motors Building across the street, but the Fisher Building is certainly an effective foil, and its massing (figs. 57, 58) and grand interior concourses (fig. 59) are undeniably handsome.

The source for the exterior treatment was undoubtedly Eliel Saarinen's Tribune Tower design of 1922. As one of Kahn's daughters recalls, "Father had by this time become a friend of Saarinen's whose work in its greater external simplicity he very much admired. . . . " As early as 1923, in an address on "Problems in City Development," Kahn had said:

There is being prepared at the moment by Eliel Saarinen, a Finnish architect, a scheme for placing the Memorial Hall at the foot of Woodward Ave. and making of it a nucleus for the improvement of a goodly part of the down-town River Front. Mr. Saarinen has been the past two months guest professor at the Michigan University [the University of Michigan—he was invited by Professor Emil Lorch of the College of Architecture and Design]. He was brought into prominence by his epoch making design for the Chicago Tribune Building in the competition for which he won second prize, though entitled to first.[5]

Figure 59
The Fisher Building; main concourse
looking south to Second Avenue. The
General Motors Building appears on
Second Avenue at the left.
(Photograph courtesy of Albert Kahn
Associates.)

Figure 57
The Fisher Building, Detroit,
1927–1929; exterior from the east on
West Grand Boulevard. (Photograph
by Hedrich-Blessing, courtesy of
Albert Kahn Associates.)

Figure 58
The Fisher Building; exterior from
Second Avenue. (Photograph by
Hedrich-Blessing, courtesy of Albert
Kahn Associates.)

In 1925 Saarinen had begun his work on the Cranbrook Academy of Art and the School for Boys in Bloomfield Hills, only a few miles from Kahn's Walnut Lake summer house and a few hundred yards from Cranbrook House, which Kahn had designed in 1909. Saarinen received Kahn's support for the Cranbrook appointment. Subsequently, they became good friends, and Saarinen was a frequent dinner guest at the Kahn homes.

There are many offspring of Saarinen's Tribune Tower scheme, and, in fact, prior to the Fisher Building Kahn had done two Detroit structures in this idiom: the new Free Press Building of 1925 and the Maccabees Building of 1926–1927. Both used the grand arched entrance, the prominent ground floor (arcaded in the Maccabees Building as at Fisher), the towerlike central mass, and a cornice-free terminus. The Fisher Building, however, is a more suave performance and also more like Saarinen's tower.[6] Much of the basic treatment is similar—for example, the termination of vertical bands of fenestration by thin-edged, round-headed arches (fig. 57), the simple two-story motif at the base, the cornice relationship of the lower mass, and the emphatic corner towers with paired windows (fig. 58). The Fisher Building, however, has an advantage in its siting condition shared by few other office buildings in the United States, the Tribune Tower included. A dogleg occurs in Second Avenue as it crosses West Grand Boulevard. The tower is located nearly, though not exactly, on an axis with Second Avenue as it comes north from the heart of town, and it can be seen full front from a great distance, acting as a strong terminus to an important urban path (see fig. 58).

The building in its present form is only a part of the original plan. The existing portion was completed in February 1929, at which time an entire issue of the *American Architect* was given over to coverage of it. The article in the *American Architect* noted that

A corresponding section is to be erected at the west end of the block and a central tower some fifty stories high is to dominate the group. When entirely completed, the building will contain a floor area larger than any now existing.[7]

A generalized rendering was included to illustrate the ultimate scheme, which was forestalled by the depression. The portion completed was awarded the Silver Medal of the Architectural League of New York in April 1929.

In 1931 Kahn designed the New Center Building diagonally opposite the Fisher Building and to the northeast. The New Center Building was much smaller and more austere than either the General Motors or the Fisher Building, befitting the times in which it was built. It was the last of the triumvirate comprising Detroit's New Center.

Notes

1. Durant resigned as head of General Motors in the fall of 1920, in part as a consequence of the depression of that year. Pierre du Pont succeeded him as president, but the de facto head of the organization was the executive vice-president, Alfred P. Sloan. Sloan became president in 1923.

2. Rather surprisingly, the main interior volume of the library seems to have been modeled on the living room of the otherwise very different house that Kahn had designed for William Clements in Bay City, Michigan, in 1908.

3. Other major works by Kahn for the University of Michigan campus were the Library, the Science Building (now Natural Science Building), Betsy Barbour Women's Residence, University Hospital, the New Medical Building, the Museum, and Burton Tower.

4. Letter from Mrs. Butzel to the author, April 10, 1967.

5. "Problems in City Development," address by Albert Kahn, in the office files, undated, audience unknown. Only the reference to Saarinen's guest professorship at Michigan fixes the year as 1923.

6. Another Kahn work that reflects an influence from Saarinen is the Burton Tower for the University of Michigan (1936–1937), though its somewhat stark exterior lacks the intimacy of scale typical of the best of Saarinen's work.

7. *American Architect* 135, No. 2563 (February 1929): 212.

7
CULMINATION, 1932–1942

Economic Recovery

In 1932 Kahn had written to Ernestine from Russia that there was "very little doing at home." In fact, the market for his talents had apparently vanished; U.S. automobile production had dropped to 1,400,000 units from its 1929 high of 5,400,000, and net tangible assets had decreased by over 25 percent. Yet Kahn was at the threshold of the busiest decade of his life. In 1933 automobile production began an upswing that would continue unabated through 1938, and, though in Kahn's lifetime it never again reached the peak of 1929, new facilities were needed for several reasons.[1] Plants dilapidated beyond the possibility of renovation had to be replaced. Others in sound condition were poorly planned for exploitation of new techniques that were essential in the lean depression years. In these cases demolition or sale of the old plant and construction of a new one were necessary to economic survival. This was particularly true of the multistory plants that had been built during the twenties by manufacturers who had not seen the logic of Ford policies at Rouge. Finally, the depression brought some changes in the relative standings of different makes and manufacturers. Most small-volume firms and those that were making only prestige cars had been forced from the field,[2] the major exception being Packard, which saved itself by introducing the more austere and much cheaper Light Eight. On the other hand, companies whose production already included low-priced lines began to commit a much larger proportion of their production to those lines and to utility vehicles. Plymouth is a case in point. It was introduced in 1928 as a by-product of the take-over of Dodge by the Chrysler Corporation. It played a minor role in total output in 1928 and 1929, but in the thirties it ranked third in popularity among all makes. Both Chrysler Corporation and General Motors in the thirties gained larger shares of the market than Ford, the leader in the twenties. Thus many manufacturers needed new facilities because of changes in their relative importance within the industry.

The revision and reactiviation of the automobile industry, then, meant renewed demand for Kahn's services. The needs of the growing aircraft industry added to this demand. The airplane's potential had been dramatized by such flights as Lindbergh's in 1927 and Wiley Post's in 1932.

In the thirties commercial uses seemed broader than ever before, and military minds became obsessed with the airplane as a war machine. *The Aircraft Year Book* of 1936 noted that Hitler's rearmament plans included an "air force [which] could back up anything that Germany might want to do."[3] By 1937 the *Year Book* noted as "most significant . . . the breakneck race of all the other large nations for military supremacy."[4] By 1938 the situation was even more tense. The first paragraph of that *Year Book* described the conditions at the time:

> At the beginning of 1938 all the principal powers of the world were striving to lead in the race for supremacy in the air, and in whatever light one might view it the goal was plainly apparent. It lay in attaining dominant air force strength, complete mastery of the air in preparation for a war that seemed to become more imminent with each passing month.[5]

The first five chapters were then entirely given over to military uses of air power. For these reasons, 1933, the low year of aircraft production, was followed by growth even more dramatic than that of the automobile industry. The year 1936 surpassed any year of the twenties; 1937 brought record peacetime sales, exceeding $100 million for the first time, and up by 50 percent over 1936; and from 1938 onward through the war, each year brought a comparable increase in airplane production.

Thus, within a year of the closing of the branch in Russia, Kahn was beginning to receive a trickle of industrial commissions. By 1935 the firm was thriving again, and toward the end of the decade and into the forties it was operating at an uprecedented pace with a staff of from 400 to 600.

Office Structure and Organization

The organizational format continued to provide specialized expertise in all aspects of the work. Albert Kahn was assisted in administration by his brothers Louis and Moritz; serving them directly was the secretarial staff. The remainder of the firm was divided into two divisions, the Technical and the Executive. The Technical Division had responsibility for carrying the work to signed construction contract. It was subdivided into four specialized departments: design, architectural, structural, and mechanical; of these all but design were again subdivided. Under the architectural department were subdivisions for industrial and commercial buildings; within the structural department were subdivisions for structural steel and reinforced concrete; the mechanical department contained subdivisions for sanitation, heating, air conditioning, electrical engineering, and process engineering. Production of specifications was carried on in a subdepartment in contact with all four technical departments. Where the Technical Division's responsibilities ended, those of the Executive Division began. It was responsible for execution of work from signed contract drawings to actual occupancy by the client and was therefore divided into two departments, one for internal office management including maintenance of correspondence and records and the other for actual field supervision.[6] There was no part of the work for which provision had not been made in the office organization—this staff was capable of dealing with data and determinants for all aspects of the building design and of seeing it through construction to the time of occupancy without the aid of any consultants. Process layouts, however, were still left in the client's hands. Though a process engineering subdivision is noted in the firm, it must have served primarily as liaison. As late as 1940 Kahn made it clear that he believed the client was inevitably and necessarily more informed than the architect about the processes used in his industry, and that it would be inefficient and pointless to attempt to duplicate this expertise.

> . . . We plainly tell our clients that we can advise as to the type of building that will best suit their requirements, but we are not process engineers. We, of course, are glad to help with suggestions and can explain how others in the same work carry on, but we do not pretend to make layouts for machinery or other equipment.[7]

Kahn's energy in managing this office became legendary. It may seem difficult to believe that he could have assumed any degree of personal control over individual projects in a firm of such size, and the problem was made still more difficult by the fact that for any given project work went forward simultaneously in all departments, demanding more or less simultaneous contact with several people in several fields of expertise. But the consensus of those who were members of the firm at that time is that he did maintain that control. His hand was felt directly in his personal early sketches for each major project. Furthermore, those who worked with him recall that in the architectural and design departments he was able to give critiques of work at each board several times a week.[8] Because of the volume of work handled by the office, the maintenance of this schedule required unusual mental and physical energy, but Kahn was known to have had that even in his days with Mason and Rice. An interviewer in 1929 described a "coatless, acrobatic figure, with its upstanding hair, moving with almost incredible celerity, buoyantly from one group to another. Nobody sprang to attention as it paused, but everyone attended."[9]

Development of each project proceeded in what can only be called seminars, guided by Kahn and including representatives of all the various pertinent skills. This was the point at which his team concept, and his view of himself as quarterback or conductor, found application. Unlike the head of the usual name office, he seems not to have brought to these seminars his concept already prepared, expecting to bend the skills of other fields toward its execution. His approach instead was to draw from the pertinent specialists the determining considerations for the issue at hand; from these considerations the concept would emerge. Thus the concept was a consequence and not a point of departure.

Others in the twentieth century, most notably Walter Gropius, have extolled the team approach to design, and of course most large firms in architecture have included a certain diversity of talents. But Kahn utilized the team concept in actual practice with a uniquely clear view of its usefulness and with a unique approach to its method of operation. He saw that a team was not simply a group of architects, or architects plus helpers, but a group of men representing all interest areas involved in factory design, and that if the factory was to work really well, all these interest areas had to be listened to. Therefore he did not consult the other areas of expertise only after the decisions had been made. Instead these other fields became integrally woven into the design process. He was so insistent on this interweaving of abilities, in fact, that, as already mentioned, graduate architects, normally the prime ingredient of an architectural firm, were actually excluded from 1920 to 1935 because of Kahn's conviction that they could not wholeheartedly participate in such an interaction.

Since we now have seen Kahn's organizational approach in its final form and in some detail, we can try to assess its advantages. Kahn described some of them in an address to the New York State Association of Architects on September 27, 1940:

> . . . The average architect, without the assistance of men who can deal with the structural problem, the sanitary, power, sprinkler, heating and ventilating, and cooling problems, is apt to fail. It is imperative that groups of men conversant with these fields join in the handling of an industrial plant. Nor is it sufficient that the architect tell the owner that he expects to call in specialists to help at the proper time. The main subjects must have consideration from the outset, the very first conference. All must work in close touch with each other to gain the desired results expeditiously; wherefore the combination must exist at the outset.[10]

He might have said more. Through Kahn's guidance of the work in frequent seminars at which pertinent areas of expertise were present, a solution was evolved as a response to, not one, but all pertinent determinants. It was not necessary, for example, to arrive at a structural scheme on the basis of structural criteria alone and then, later, attempt to modify it to fit the needs of light admission. Since both the light admission criteria and the structural criteria were immediately available, under Kahn's guidance and coordination the scheme could evolve from simultaneous consideration of both. This method had a number of advantages: it meant a minimum of backtracking and change within the office, which saved money for the client because the plant was under construction, and therefore in production, sooner; and it was of benefit to Kahn because it meant that fees were not spent negatively on physical and mental erasing. Furthermore, it meant that the building itself was particularly apt to be highly economical. Adaptation of a single concept to other purposes is not likely to lead to an optimal or efficient solution, and this is exactly what Kahn's design process avoided. The solution as conceived in the presence of all criteria involved a minimum of subsequent compromise and adjustment. Finally, and perhaps most important of all, Kahn's approach meant a philosophical and operational commitment to the serious inclusion of all determinants, so that it was highly unlikely that the building w

be deficient with respect to any of them.

The Formulated Approach: The Chevrolet Commercial Body Plant

Typical of the early postdepression work of the office is the Chevrolet Commercial Body Plant in Indianapolis, plans for which were issued September 20, 1935. The site is to the west of the White River Parkway on Henry Street. A number of comparatively small two-story brick-walled mill construction buildings were demolished to make way for the new factory. This factory is a textbook example of certain principles of planning enumerated by Moritz Kahn, speaking for the firm, in 1929.

> For general purposes, a standardized plan of building will prove to be of advantage. This refers particularly to such buildings as are used for motor assembly plants, or for the manufacture of bodies, motor parts, machine tools . . . and the like. In this type of factory the architect need only familiarize himself with the general method of manufacture, and the building need not be designed for any particular installation of equipment. There are other types of factory buildings, however, such as foundries, forge shops, cement plants and the like which must be designed to fit particular schemes of equipment installation.[11]

Obviously the Chevrolet Plant is of the first type. Consequently it is a large, flexible loft space, whose basic requirements the office had reduced to formula at least six years before.

> Column spacings for single-story buildings should fall in the range of from 25 feet to 40 feet center to center. . . . Single-story buildings, in general, should have a clear height of 14 feet to the under side of the roof trusses. This dimension, of course, does not take into consideration clearances for overhead cranes or conveyors which will require special treatment.[12]

The main portion of the building is 1,122 feet by 322 feet, with an ell to the southeast 400 by 280 feet in which the two high crane bays are included (figs. 60, 61). A 40 by 40-foot module establishes column centers throughout except in the crane bays where columns are on 20-foot centers east to west and 80 feet north to south (fig. 61). Height to the bottom of trusses is 14 feet 3 inches in typical bays, 40 feet in crane bays. Typical bays are spanned by Warren trusses with doubly tapered top chords above which a superstructure, resting at the central and outside panel points, supports monitor sash and the upper roof level. Over the railroad spur welded steel bent beams, similar to those of the Ford Engineering Laboratory, provide additional headroom. Over the crane bays a Pratt truss with a span of 80 feet supports a monitor system slightly modified from that of the rest of the building (figs. 62, 63). Resistance to racking is provided by the usual method of X bracing in walls and between the upper chords of the trusses. A concrete slab subfloor is used throughout. This is surfaced with end-grain wood blocks that are more easily maintained than concrete, do not damage tools, and do not produce an abrasive dust. Unit heaters are suspended between trusses (fig. 64).

A cafeteria, two transformer and switchboard rooms, and six toilet rooms are in mezzanine structures that have a trussed flat roof. The toilet rooms are smaller than those of earlier work but are placed at closer intervals, the object being the reduction of employee travel time. Again to quote Moritz Kahn:

> Locker rooms and toilet rooms in expansive plants should not be concentrated in a few large units, but should be divided into many small units located around the plant so that the distances between them are not too great and to avoid excessive loss of time in their use by employees. In a single-story building, spread over a large area, toilet and locker rooms can with advantage, be located on elevated platforms in the spaces between the roof trusses.[13]

Outer walls are of brick up to the concrete windowsill, above which is continuous steel sash. Gunite sheathes the upper walls at the monitor ends.

The Chevrolet Plant represents an evolution from the best features of Kahn's factories of the twenties. In particular, the simple roof scheme of the Glenn Martin plant of 1929, descended from the Ford Engineering Laboratory, has been grafted to the simple wall treatment of the Rouge Motor Assembly Building. The Chevrolet Plant has six corners, five exterior and one reentrant. Of the exterior corners two are high, and three are low. The structural condition within the two high corners is, of course, different from that of the low corners, but since the sash

Figure 60
Chevrolet Motor Division
Commercial Body Plant,
Indianapolis, 1935; aerial view.
(Photograph courtesy of Albert Kahn
Associates.)

Figure 61
Chevrolet Commercial Body Plant;
plan. (Photograph by Graydon
Miller, courtesy of Albert Kahn
Associates.)

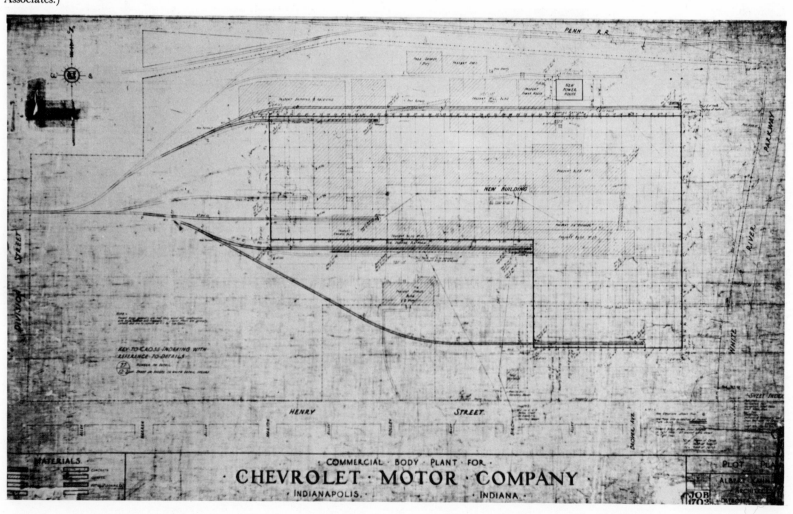

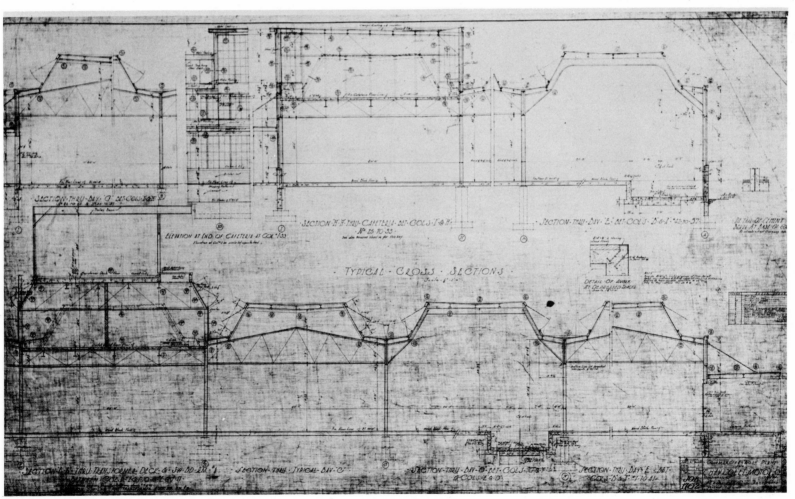

Figure 62
Chevrolet Commercial Body Plant;
typical sections. (Photograph by
Graydon Miller, courtesy of Albert
Kahn Associates.)

Figure 63
Chevrolet Commercial Body Plant;
section through crane bays.
(Photograph by Graydon Miller,
courtesy of Albert Kahn Associates.)

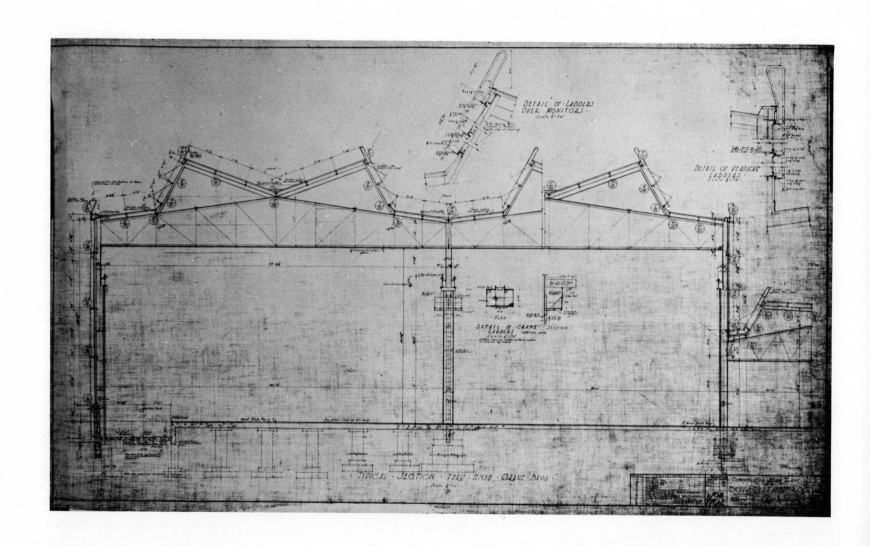

Figure 64
Chevrolet Commercial Body Plant;
interior. (Photograph courtesy of
Albert Kahn Associates.)

is a part of an independent curtain lying outside the structural cage, the sash corner details are identical. The one reentrant corner is also nearly identical—the 4-inch by 4-inch steel angle that receives the sash is simply reversed—all other conditions remain unchanged. Such details make the building easy to bid, quick and foolproof in construction, and therefore highly economical.

The relationship between the Chevrolet Plant and Moritz Kahn's statements of 1929 has been stressed to point out that the firm had to some degree been able to reduce its experience to a formula, to standardize an approach, and to develop some basic criteria of wide applicability. The office did not pursue innovation except as called for in the nature of the problem. Effort could be specifically concentrated on areas of dysfunction. The advantages are clear: the office would have had a sense of direction and purpose, and the building would have received study where it needed it most. This modus operandi no doubt also applies to earlier periods of the office and can be inferred from the examples at the Ford Highland Park or Rouge plants. It has been discussed at this point because after Moritz Kahn's comments in 1929 the situation can be clearly established. To some extent it is analogous to the creation of a style, which establishes a common vocabulary of approach to a more or less diverse series of problems. Kahn's situation, however, was unique in two ways. First, the "vocabulary" was expressible in relatively specific form, as Moritz Kahn's comments, cited earlier, demonstrate ("For general purposes . . . column spacings . . . of from 25 feet to 40 feet [and] a clear height of 14 feet . . . "). Second, the "style" was quantifiably testable in terms of speed of construction, dollar cost, illumination of the working plane, numbers of manufacturing processes per unit of floor area, costs of operation and maintenance, and costs of change.

The relationship between Kahn's methods and those of his clients, particularly Henry Ford, has been suggested previously in discussions of Kahn's early office organization and organizational self-sufficiency. Without belaboring the point, it might also be suggested that Kahn's reduction of his designs to formulas has analogies, though indirect, in manufacturing processes. Did such concepts as the assembly line, interchangeable parts, standardized models, and extensive production runs begin to infuse his mental processes and to generate a related conception of building design?

The De Soto Press Shop

The Wyoming Avenue (Detroit) Press Shop for the De Soto Division of Chrysler Corporation, dated seven months after Chevrolet Indianapolis, is a similar scheme. The basic plan module is again 40 feet by 40 feet, halved and doubled where processes of manufacture, or equipment needs, dictate, as along the west edge and in the press area to the southeast (see fig. 66). Clear heights are similar to those at Chevrolet. Heating and wind bracing are also similar, and the building is typically clad in brick, steel sash, and Gunite. At De Soto attention has been given to improving the efficiency of the truss-monitor scheme by using a truss that supports the roof with fewer pounds of steel and which, by its profile, makes possible monitor lighting with fewer additive steel members. Unlike Chevrolet, the truss profile provides for the monitor integrally (figs. 64, 67). Only the two small angle-framed "ears" are added to extend the monitor depth. A truss of this shape cannot, of course, be an exact response to loading conditions, which are more or less uniform across the span, inducing stress conditions that change gradually and therefore do not suggest an abrupt change in the truss profile. Depth in a simple span truss, however, is most useful at its mid-span; the ends, resisting shear only, can be shallow provided that they have an adequate cross-sectional area of steel. So the basic proposition of the De Soto scheme, the reduction in depth at the ends of the truss to allow inclusion of some portion of the monitor, was an essentially logical solution for this context and a promising one for future buildings. Since the extensive superstructure of Chevrolet was no longer needed, fewer pounds of steel were required per square foot covered. The changes in angle of the bottom chord of the truss are not expressed in the elevational treatment (figs. 65, 68, 70)—to have done so would have led to nonuniform sash. However, monitor ears are also not expressed in elevation, perhaps because of a need to limit flashing joints, or perhaps simply because the greater number of angles would have been inappropriately frilly.

Figure 65
De Soto Division Press Shop, Detroit,
1936; exterior of original unit.
(Photograph by Fred Eggert,
courtesy of Albert Kahn Associates.)

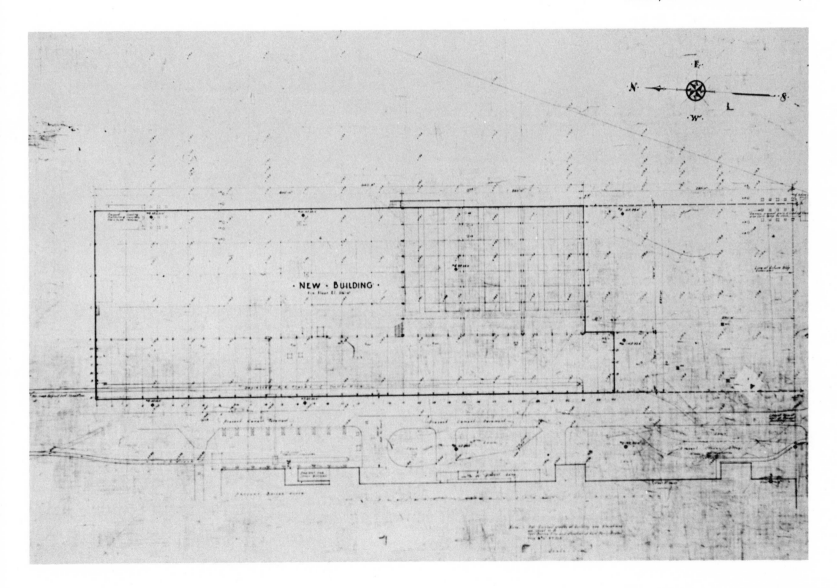

Figure 66
De Soto Press Shop; plan.
(Photograph by Graydon Miller,
courtesy of Albert Kahn Associates.)

Figure 67
De Soto Press Shop; sections.
(Photograph by Graydon Miller,
courtesy of Albert Kahn Associates.)

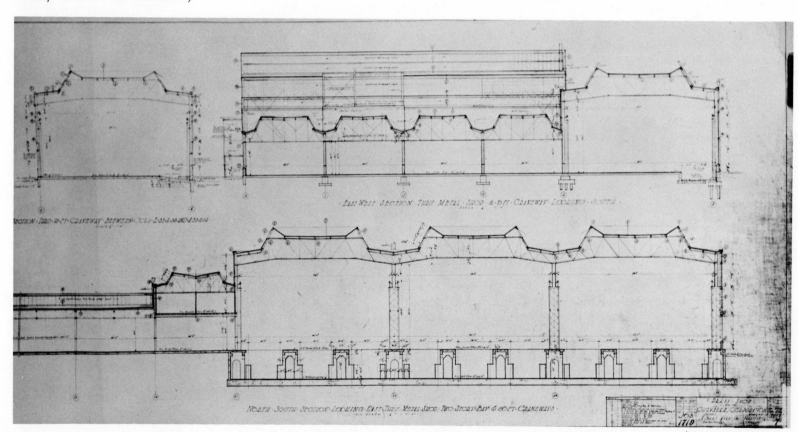

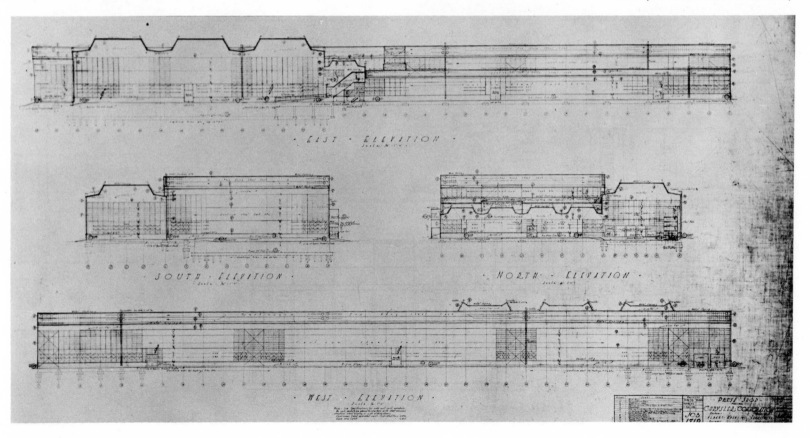

Figure 68
De Soto Press Shop; elevations.
(Photograph by Graydon Miller,
courtesy of Albert Kahn Associates.)

Figure 69
De Soto Press Shop; interior.
(Photograph by Manning Bros.,
courtesy of Albert Kahn Associates.)

Figure 70
De Soto Press Shop; exterior of 1941
addition. (Photograph by Manning
Bros., courtesy of Albert Kahn
Associates.)

The concluding work in this particular series of developments is the Curtiss-Wright Corporation's Stack Shops and Storage Building at Buffalo, New York, finished in April 1938 (fig. 71). In this building the trusses are very deep at their centers and taper to pointed ends, a virtually ideal shape for a simple-span truss (see fig. 72). They are carried on the bottom chords of continuous longitudinal trusses that transfer the forces to the columns and provide all longitudinal resistance against racking. These longitudinal trusses are of a depth equal to that of the transverse trusses at their first panel points. The monitor again requires only the small additional triangular framing. All parts are thus intrinsically efficient and all are interrelated— the exterior elevations are a direct result of this cohesive scheme. As so often happens in architecture, the final good solution to all problems seems in the end deceptively simple.

The Chrysler Half-Ton Truck Plant

The Half-Ton Truck Plant for Chrysler Corporation, at Mound and 8 Mile roads in Detroit, is probably the most frequently cited of all of Kahn's buildings. It is usually lauded for the crisp expressiveness of its form, which is seen as exemplifying a twentieth-century technological style. The plant attracts this kind of praise because it is remarkably handsome and photogenic, as shown in figure 77 (the few formal awkwardnesses of its exterior are usually avoided by the cameraman). The envelope consists of precise and elegant planar surfaces with minimal reveals throughout. The crisp forms and insistent planarity make the building itself appear to have been machined. It is, in fact, a marvelous example to cite if one is drawing analogies between function and beauty. But the real genius of the design goes deeper.

The plant consists of two buildings. To the north is the Assembly Building, 402 by 1,262 feet, and to the south across a rail spur, the Export Building, 122 by 242 feet (figs. 74, 73). Drawings for both units were issued August 14, 1937.

The Assembly Building can be regarded as consisting of three main volumes. A two-story office portion with a flat roof and brick walls is at the west end. The north side consists of a high, partly two-storied volume with a monitor roof. This is for delivery, stocks, and various subassemblies. The main body of the building is the flexible loft space visible at right in figure 73. The disposition of the three basic volumes is apparent in the elevations (fig. 75).

The key to the design lies in the roof structure of the large loft space. Bent beams at 20-foot intervals generally follow the profile of those in the Ford Engineering Laboratory of fifteen years before, but the actual structural scheme of the Half-Ton Truck Plant is completely different. Trusses at 60-foot intervals[14] carry the beams, which are suspended from the top chord, and transfer loads to columns every 40 feet; thus each bay is 40 by 60 feet, or half again the typical bay size of the Chevrolet and De Soto plants but with the same poundage of steel used per square foot. The larger size has been economically achieved by clever use of cantilevering; the upper portions of the bent beams are continuous across the trusses and cantilever 12 feet beyond each end (figs. 76, 78). The stresses in a beam used in this way are reduced to approximately those of a 40-foot simple span, so that a beam of that lighter size will support the load. The low roof is then carried on a beam of short span, actually about 30 feet, and consequently it, too, can be made of a light steel section. A light triangular frame projects upward from the upper beam (see fig. 78), and the inclined face created by this light frame and the down-turned portion of the beam is glazed to become the monitor lighting. The structural cage utilizes a minimal amount of material, and the cantilevering principle that makes this possible is exploited to provide light admission with a minimum of additional material. The upper roof space between the trusses is used for occasional mezzanine toilets and transformer rooms.

The columns support the higher portions of the structure. Though a saving in their length could be realized if they occurred under the low roof, that would be possible only if the span were doubled or the low roof were made much broader than the high one. The first alternative is untenable because 120-foot spans would be uneconomical without clear programmatic needs. The second alternative would lead to a poorly lighted zone under the low roof since monitors

Figure 71
Curtiss-Wright Corporation Stack
Shops and Storage Building, Buffalo,
New York, 1938. (Photograph
courtesy of Albert Kahn Associates.)

Figure 72
Curtiss-Wright Storage Building;
diagrammatic drawing. (Drawing by
author, photographed by Graydon
Miller.)

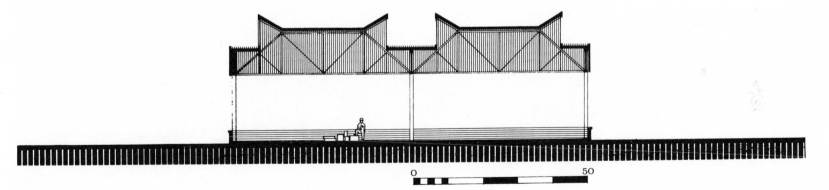

0   50

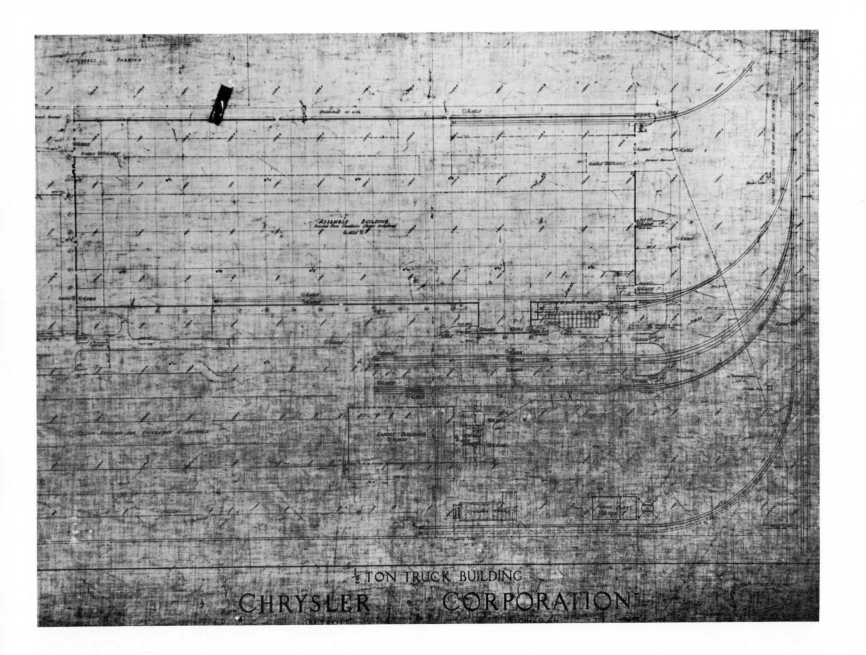

½ TON TRUCK BUILDING

CHRYSLER · CORPORATION

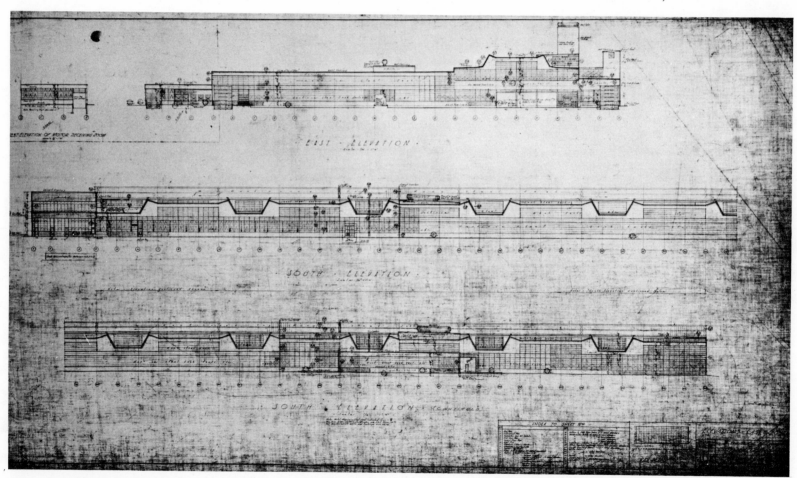

Figure 75
Chrysler Half-Ton Truck Plant;
elevations. (Photograph by Graydon
Miller, courtesy of Albert Kahn
Associates.)

Figure 76
Chrysler Half-Ton Truck Plant;
sections. (Photograph by Graydon
Miller, courtesy of Albert Kahn
Associates.)

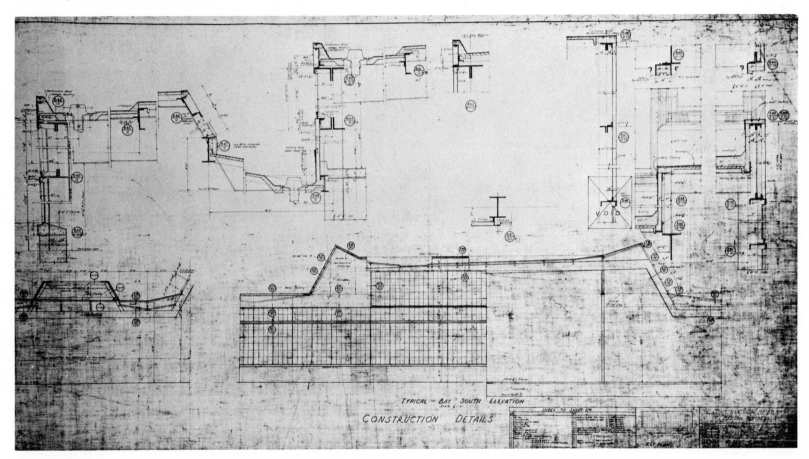

Figure 77
Chrysler Half-Ton Truck Plant;
exterior of the Export Building.
(Photograph by Hedrich-Blessing,
courtesy of Albert Kahn Associates.)

Figure 78
Chrysler Half-Ton Truck Plant;
interior of the Assembly Building.
The rail spur canopy appears
through the windows. (Photograph
by Hedrich-Blessing, courtesy of
Albert Kahn Associates.)

provide even illumination only if the low roof between them is relatively narrow. Locating columns under the low roof would have one further disadvantage in that the bottom chord of the truss would determine headroom, and the entire roof would have to be raised at least three feet.

The geometry of the cladding materials reveals the principles that lie behind the design. The cornice line follows the profile of the bent beam and its monitor ears. Fenestration is composed in rectilinear expanses for simplicity of detailing. These rectangles delineate the lower edges of the beams and the inner faces of the columns and in this way reveal the fact that the building is structured by a system of beams augmented by trusses rather than by trusses alone. The shelter for the railroad platform shows the same careful study (fig. 73). The roof, which is carried on columns along the centerline of the platform, cantilevers on triangular trusses extending over the vehicle and railroad sides of the platform. The difference in required clearance height on each side has been respected by reversing the truss triangle; on the railroad side the top chord is horizontal, and on the vehicle side, the bottom chord. Each horizontal plane of the shelter in turn meets the upper or lower edge of the canopy connecting the two main buildings.

The exterior also reflects Kahn's intuitive tendencies toward a nonterminated architecture, tendencies that first appeared in his early multistory concrete factories. The elevations of the Half-Ton Truck Plant appear to be no more than the result of slicing it off at that particular length. There is no predetermined compositional terminus; the entire conception derives from his long-standing acceptance of indeterminate extension. The Half-Ton Truck Plant is properly considered a masterpiece of industrial architecture. No other general manufacturing building of its date and of equal sophistication has come to light.

Yet its very sophistication may have brought some unforeseen problems, because the scheme was not used again by Kahn in quite the same way. The forms, however, were seductive, perhaps too much so, since they were repeated verbatim a year later for the Ohio Steel Foundry at Lima but without the structure that led to them. The Steel Foundry's structure is of simple flat trusses without cantilevers, the columns occurring directly under the peaks of the monitors.[15] From the outside the appearance is nearly identical to the Chrysler Export Building (though a bit heavier and more ponderous in proportions), but from the inside the relationship between envelope and structure makes no sense.

The Glenn Martin Assembly Building

Nineteen thirty-seven was a vintage year for the Kahn office. In addition to the Chrysler Half-Ton Truck Plant the firm also designed a remarkable new Assembly Building for the Glenn L. Martin Company's plant north of Baltimore. On April 14, plans were issued for the new structure to be built contiguous to the 1929 unit (fig. 79). Martin conceived this Assembly Building as a single, column-free space 300 by 450 feet in plan. He was convinced that within the expected life of the building, airplanes would be built with wingspans approaching 300 feet, and it seemed to him poor planning to build a factory that could not be adapted to their construction. And if the interior were to house a plane of 300-foot wingspread, obviously the plane must get out; one entire end of the building would have to be a door. So the plan was clear at the outset—a 300- by 450-foot rectangle, one end of which could be entirely opened (fig. 80).

Kahn's purpose was to derive the logical physical structure. An interoffice competition of sorts was held among several design squads preparing different proposals, and alternatives were weighed, literally. The lightest design, in pounds of steel per square foot of roof supported, was chosen—a scheme of simple span, parallel chord Pratt trusses, 300 feet in length, 30 feet in depth, placed at 50-foot intervals.

No building had been built with a flat span as great as 300 feet. The largest was the 240-foot span of the Crucible Steel Company mill of 1919 at Harrison, New Jersey. In the 1890s a number of train sheds had been built whose approximately flat trusses were of the order of 200 feet. The largest train-shed span, however, that of the Broad Street Station in Philadelphia, used the arch principle to cross its 300 feet 8 inches. On the other hand, much longer flat spans had been used in bridge construction for many decades. The first all-steel bridge in America, for example, the Chicago and Alton Railroad Bridge at Glasgow, Missouri, had spans of 314 feet.

By the time of the Glenn Martin project, spans much greater than this were common in bridge work. Furthermore, the Martin design assumed live loads—that is, superimposed loads other than those of the building itself—of 30 pounds per square foot (typical for the Kahn office) or 1,500 pounds per lineal foot of truss, which of course was far less than the loading for any bridge. Logically Kahn turned to bridge techniques for the Martin trusses.

Upper and lower chords of the great 300-foot trusses consist of pairs of built-up 20-inch-deep channels spread 18 inches apart, back to back. A 30-inch-wide closing plate is riveted across the bottom of the lower chord and the top of the upper. Verticals and diagonals are also made up of a pair of like members, held a few inches apart by a latticework web.

The great depth and wide spacing of the main trusses suggested the use of monitors running parallel with them, admitting light through the flanks of the trusses (fig. 81). Accordingly, the 50-foot Warren secondary trusses, equal to the primary structure of most factories, support a roof surface that occurs alternately at the top and near the bottom of the main trusses. The 19-foot-high vertical plane created in this way is glazed. The monitor sash is framed out 8 feet from the face of the truss in order to reduce the width of the low roof and thereby give more even illumination. Similar glazing occurs at the ends of the building; through it the great trusses can be seen from the exterior (see figs. 82, 83, 84). Lateral forces are countered by the usual X bracing in walls and between trusses (figs. 85, 86).

Airplane assembly is not done on a moving assembly line. The planes are located at station points on the assembly room floor, and the men climb to various parts of the plane to perform assembly processes by hand. In the case of large aircraft this means that the men work at a number of different heights in the assembly space. Because of this and because of the great height of the room, the usual unit heaters are not used; the blower force needed to produce warmth near the floor would have to be so great as to cause real discomfort at higher levels. Two large heater rooms are located under the floor. They feed outlets located near the outside wall. Return air is handled by a trench and grilles along the centerline of the building. Toilets and lockers,

Figure 79
Glenn L. Martin Company Plant,
Middle River, Maryland, 1929–;
rendering of the proposed ultimate
scheme. The original 1929 unit is at
right center, the Assembly Building
of 1937 immediately to its left. The
1939 manufacturing unit is next left;
to the rear is a Navy Assembly unit
of 1941. (Photograph courtesy of
Albert Kahn Associates.)

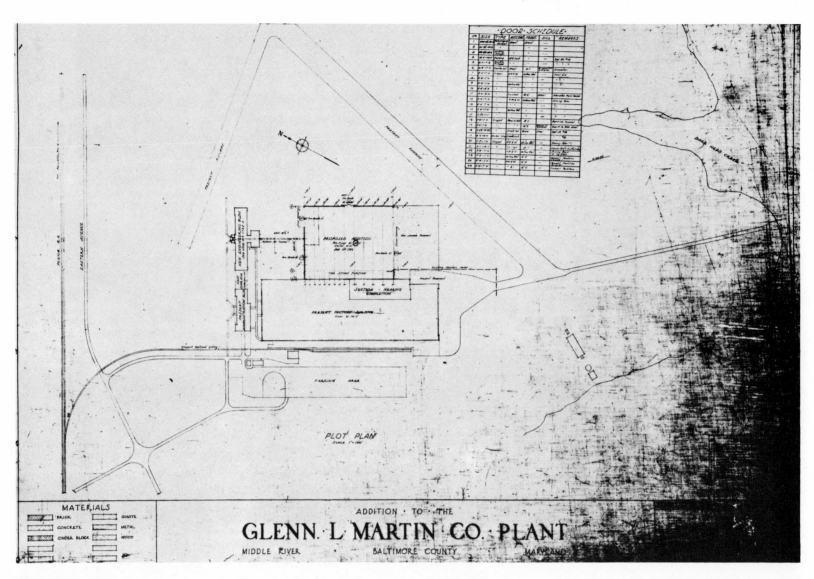

Figure 80
Glenn Martin Assembly Building,
1937; plan. (Photograph by Graydon
Miller, courtesy of Albert Kahn
Associates.)

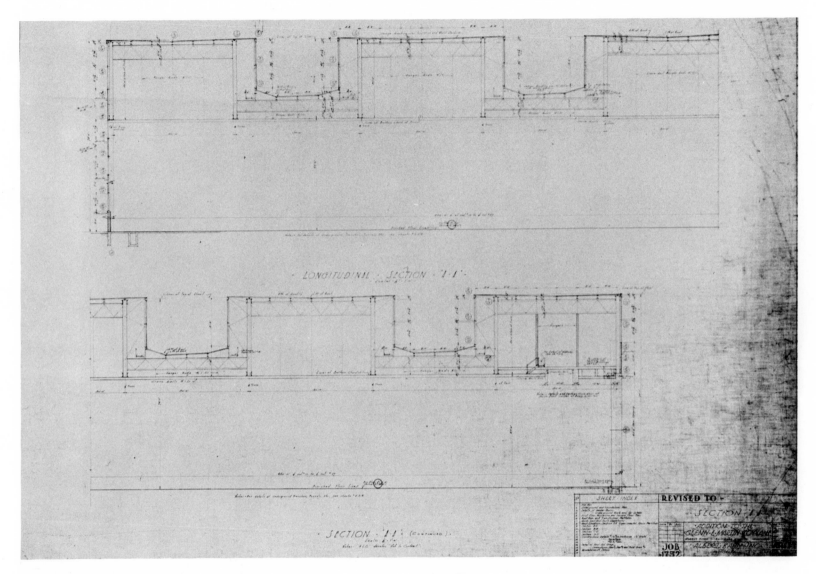

Figure 81
Glenn Martin Assembly Building;
sections. (Photograph by Graydon
Miller, courtesy of Albert Kahn
Associates.)

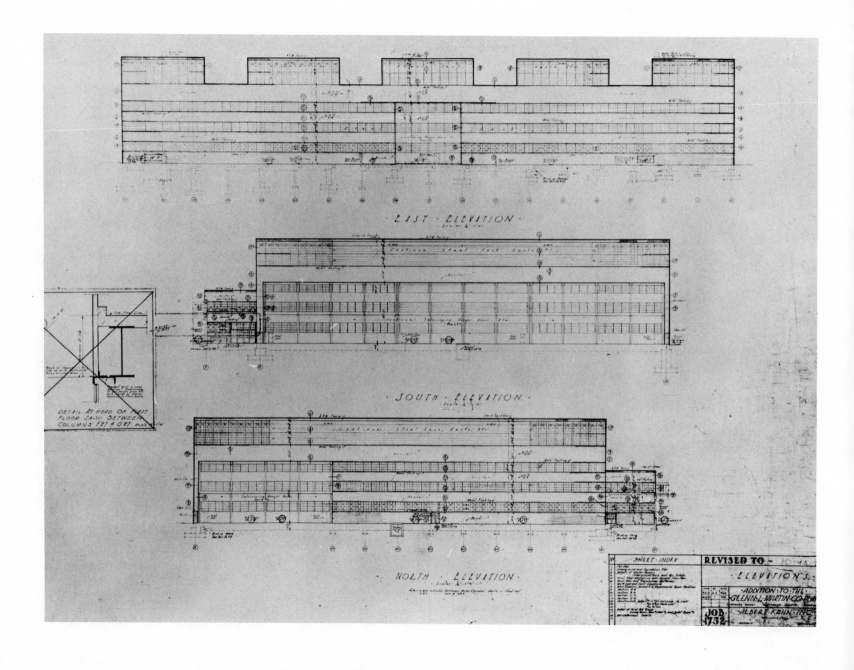

EAST · ELEVATION ·

SOUTH · ELEVATION ·

DETAIL AT HEAD OF FIRST
FLOOR SASH BETWEEN
COLUMNS F21 & G21

NORTH · ELEVATION ·

SHEET · INDEX

REVISED TO -

ELEVATIONS

ADDITION TO THE
GLENN · L · MARTIN · CO ·

ALBERT · KAHN · INC ·

JOB
1752

Figure 82
Glenn Martin Assembly Building; elevations. (Photograph by Graydon Miller, courtesy of Albert Kahn Associates.)

Figure 83
Glenn Martin Plant; exterior of the Assembly Building, with Administration Building to the right front. (Photograph by Forster Studio, courtesy of Albert Kahn Associates.)

Figure 84
Glenn Martin Plant; exterior of the
Assembly Building facing the
airfield, showing the full-width door.
(Photograph courtesy of Albert Kahn
Associates.)

Figure 85
Glenn Martin Plant; airfield facade
and interior of the Assembly
Building. (Photograph by Damora,
courtesy of Albert Kahn Associates.)

Figure 86
Glenn Martin Plant; interior of the
Assembly Building. (Photograph
courtesy of Albert Kahn Associates.)

supervision, first aid, and so forth, are located in a two-story 39-foot-wide annex along the west wall. This in turn abuts the east face of the 1929 structure.

At the airfield end is the door, 299 feet 11 inches wide and 45 feet high (see figs. 84, 85), divided into three sections horizontally and two vertically, and operable as separate sections or as a unit. Its treatment is carefully repetitive of the rest of the building; figures 84 and 85 show the jambs between window runs, which have been carefully painted darker to preserve the visual continuity of the strip.

The impact of the vast interior space is difficult to describe or photograph. The monitor projections alone are far larger in height and width than the typical bays of the Chevrolet Plant at Indianapolis. The scale is magnificent. As William MacDonald has said of the Pantheon, the space swallows up human gestures. The exterior is a handsomely concise statement of the underlying scheme, with no overstudied or fussy elements to disturb the grandness of the immense structure.

The building was used to assemble the PBM Mariner and the PB2M Mars, the largest plane to serve in World War II. By 1943 the latter had a wingspan of over 200 feet and was, no doubt, the sort of plane Martin had had in mind six years earlier.

The Glenn Martin Addition, 1939

On February 5, 1939, Kahn received a telephone call from Glenn Martin requesting still another addition, a contiguous manufacturing unit of 440,000 square feet to be ready for use by May 1. This was the most demanding schedule that Kahn or anyone else had ever faced. The self-containment of the organization, valuable before, was now indispensable.

> . . . The morning after Mr. Martin's telephone call, I was in Baltimore with an architectural assistant, a structural designer, and an estimator. That day, we prepared a number of schemes of plan and construction, showing the comparative steel tonnage. . . . The next day we called in steel contractors. . . . the next day we placed the contracts. . . .
> To save time in building, we planned to make the construction below the first floor level of reinforced concrete . . . which incidentally was entirely in place ready for the structural steel the day this was delivered. We placed contracts for the ground floor construction within eleven days

from the day we were called in. . . . Without a complete organization, all starting at the same time, this record could not have been achieved. Group practice is essential for such a result. . . . [16]

Not only was group practice within the office essential; there must also have been a great deal of rapport, familiarity, and common language between the architect and the contractor. Contracts placed so quickly must have been based on verbal and sketch information plus a great deal of intuition and shared experience, and this in turn would presume that the architect was nearly as familiar with contracting as the contractor himself and that both had a consummate grasp of engineering. All skills of the firm were clearly utilized to the fullest. Designers, engineers, and administrators in intimate collaboration and in conjunction with the contractor had to make instantaneous and correct decisions. This was possible only because of unmatched, virtually intuitive familiarity with the problems involved. Administration and business procedures in scheduling, placement of orders, timing of shipments, and so forth, also had to proceed with absolute smoothness, and it is apparent that they did. The building was completed on April 23, with the necessary million dollars' worth of equipment installed and ready for use. Production began four days later, or three days in advance of the deadline, and seventy-seven days from the original telephone call.

The *Engineering News-Record* commented at the time (June 22, 1939) that "the new building is not a notable structure from the standpoint of design innovations." That may be true, if the word "innovations" is meant in the literal sense. On the other hand, the design is a fresh and efficient use of familiar elements. Warren trusses supported at their midpoints and cantilevering in either direction comprise the basic scheme, a scheme that is again more common to bridge construction than to architecture. Since they taper toward their ends, the profile they create is nicely suited to the monitor form (see fig. 88). These trusses in turn rest on trusses running east and west, spanning 100 feet between columns.

The total plant (fig. 87) is one of Kahn's finest designs. Though smaller than many others, it deals with the making of machines at a scale unprecedented even in his own work. The

Figure 87
Glenn Martin Plant; exterior
showing the complex in 1939.
(Photograph courtesy of Albert Kahn
Associates.)

Figure 88
Glenn Martin Plant; sections
through 1939 addition. (Photograph
by Graydon Miller, courtesy of
Albert Kahn Associates.)

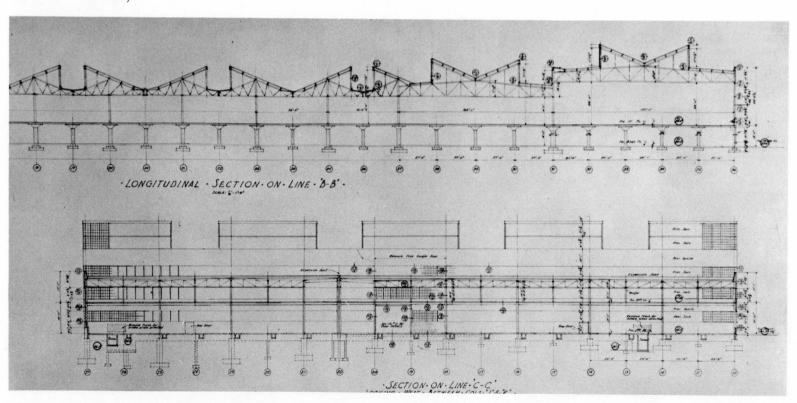

·LONGITUDINAL ·SECTION· ON· LINE· ·B-B·

·SECTION· ON· LINE· ·C-C·

principles behind every aspect of the design are conservative; the power of the solution lies in the exploitation of these principles at a scale and with a boldness normally found only in great works of civil engineering, from which in fact the principles were drawn. The uninterrupted sweep of the airfield, with the Atlantic beyond, provides an appropriately grand setting.

Two years later and a mile to the east, Kahn designed Martin plant number two at Middle River. For this second plant, to build the B-26 Marauder, he repeated almost verbatim the various portions of the original complex and in the same year used the basic scheme again for a third Martin plant at Omaha, Nebraska.

World War II: The Chrysler Tank Arsenal

As American industry became increasingly involved in the production of war weapons, the pressure on the Kahn firm grew proportionately. From December 1939 to December 1942 the government alone commissioned the office to design $200 million worth of construction, and until at least December 1941 this was supplemented by the usual volume of work from private industry.[17] Under this load the staff, growing in size throughout the thirties, reached a maximum of over 600 members. Schedules of the sort cited earlier became commonplace. Kahn commented on the process of war plant design:

> Even before definite commitments are made . . . the respective manufacturers have spent night and day on process layouts and the architects and engineers have been called in to prepare tentative schemes for properly housing their equipment.
> With contracts definitely placed, not a moment can be lost. The type of building best suited has been decided upon; so has the floor space required. Often within less than a week's time, the structural steel drawings must be developed sufficiently to obtain competitive prices ready for placing contracts. Supplying the steel frame, obtaining the necessary material, much of which must come from the mills, and fabricating it are the bottlenecks. . . .
> To save time, we must exercise care in employing structural shapes most readily obtainable. . . . And to speed up deliveries, substitutions must often be made to suit the company's stock piles or rollings of the mills. Standardization, as far as possible, is all-important, and so is simplicity of construction.
> To accomplish the necessary results requires an organization keyed up to the situation, thoroughly experienced so that decisions may be immediate and accurate, and production must be just about machinelike. . . . [18]

This was the process used in the design and construction of the Chrysler Tank Arsenal in Detroit.

In June 1940 William S. Knudsen, as head of an advisory committee of the Council of National Defense, directed Chrysler to plan for the production of tanks, which had not been previously produced as a quantity project. The Chrysler staff went to the Rock Island, Illinois, arsenal to see a tank. They had never seen one before, but that was only the beginning of their difficulties. At Rock Island they saw the M2Al, without armor. Two weeks later they were told that a new M3 General Grant would replace the M2Al, and the arsenal should be designed to produce the M3. But the M3 itself was not yet designed; its design was fully resolved only after the plant was in production and it, in turn, was abandoned after one year. Such difficulties are easily forgotten, but they were certainly excruciating at the time. From this morass of noninformation the Chrysler staff tried to get some sense of the industrial process involved. Plant engineers attempted to determine or to create the equipment necessary. They and the executive staff determined as best they could the flow patterns, space and light requirements, and the consequent size and configuration of the plant. In the end their criteria were, no doubt, vague, and Kahn was probably instructed to design a plant with maximum flexibility and minimal foreseeable obstructions; in any event this was what he did. Plans were issued September 16, 1940, and construction began a week later.

The site is in Warren Township seventeen miles outside Detroit, on Van Dyke Avenue between 11 and 12 Mile roads. One hundred and thirteen acres of farmland were purchased adjacent to the Michigan Central Railroad, from which a siding and spur were run. The factory itself is 520 feet across the east face (fig. 89) and 1,380 feet in depth east to west (fig. 90). The rail spur runs the full length of the building, stopping just short of the open door at the end of the longitudinal bay. This delivery bay is 60 feet wide; from its flank open twenty-three subassembly bays also each 60 feet wide. They, in turn, are terminated by the east-west final assembly bay, which is 80 feet wide and runs the entire length of the building; this bay is visible at the far left in figure 89 (see also section, fig. 91). The plan is thus an abstraction of the rudiments

Figure 89
Chrysler Corporation Tank Arsenal,
Detroit, 1941; exterior from the
northeast. The railroad spur runs
through the entire length of the
building and terminates just short of
the door at right. The high unit at
far left is the assembly bay; the
monitored bays perpendicular to it
enclose secondary operations.
(Photograph courtesy of Albert Kahn
Associates.)

Figure 90
Chrysler Tank Arsenal; plan.
(Photograph by Graydon Miller,
courtesy of Albert Kahn Associates.)

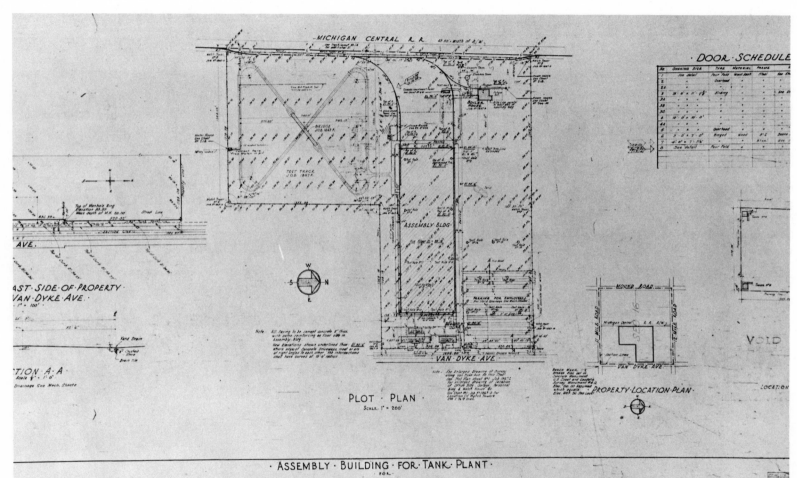

Figure 91
Chrysler Tank Arsenal; transverse
section looking east. (Photograph by
Graydon Miller, courtesy of Albert
Kahn Associates.)

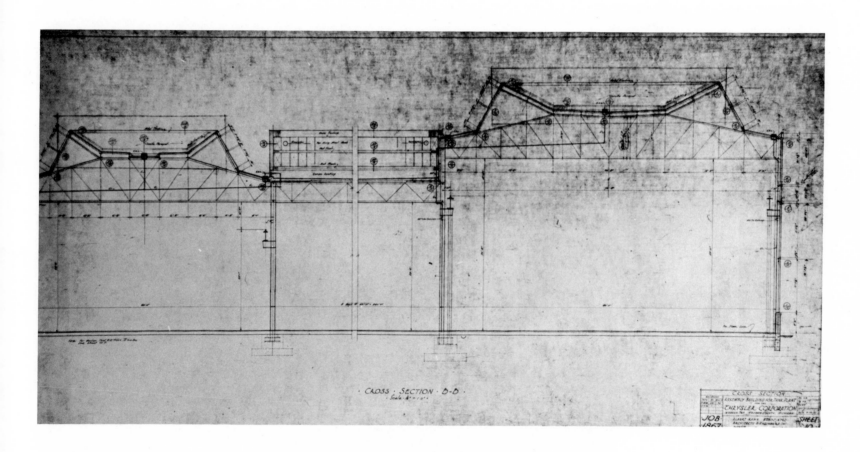

Figure 92
Chrysler Tank Arsenal; interior of
final assembly area. The tank shown
is the M3 General Grant, produced
until July 1942. (Photograph
courtesy of Albert Kahn Associates.)

of manufacture: raw materials arrive along the north face and are processed in a southerly direction through the body of the building; subassemblies are then sequentially assembled in a linear progression along the south face. Raw material enters the northwest corner; the finished product leaves the southwest corner.

The structure is similar to that of the Curtiss-Wright Storage Building, though the ends of the Pratt trusses are not pointed and each bears on its own set of columns, rather than on a perpendicular truss system (figs. 91, 92). Clear heights to the bottom of trusses are 29 feet and 39 feet. Wall sash reaches the line of the cornice on the long side and continues at this height on the monitor ends also, so that a part of the truss zone is glazed and a part is opaque. As a result, the natural light quality is exceptionally good, though one could argue that the exterior treatment is a less direct reflection of the building structure.

The scheme is of the general manufacturing loft space type but with clear spans and heights that are larger than usual and an exceptionally clean plan-process relationship. The usefulness and efficiency of this scheme were quickly demonstrated. The arsenal produced its first tank on Good Friday of 1941 before the plant itself was entirely complete and five months ahead of schedule, thus providing the ultimate example of a factory that yields its product at the earliest possible moment. The original request from the Army was for a total output of 1,500 M3 General Grant units; 1,300 were produced in the first year alone, at which time the plant was expanded by an addition of 450 feet toward the railroad and an additional 100-foot-wide assembly bay running the entire new length of 1,830 feet. The plant was then con verted to produce the M4 Sherman and later the Pershing tanks. By the war's end 25,059 tanks had been built there. This was the first factory of the war to receive the Army-Navy "E" award for production excellence, conferred on August 10, 1942. Tanks from the arsenal equipped many allied armies including the army of Field Marshal Montgomery in North Africa. Thus the five-month gain in the completion of the arsenal was of pivotal importance to the war. Winston Churchill said of Montgomery's actions in North Africa "the Grants [M3's, most of them from the first month of

Figure 93
Amertorp Corporation Torpedo
Plant, Chicago, 1942. (Photograph
courtesy of Albert Kahn Associates.)

production] and the Lees stopped Rommel at El Alamein; the Shermans defeated him." This opinion was reiterated by Field Marshal Sir John Dill: "Had it not been for . . . Detroit, the battle of El Alamein might never have been won—or even fought." At the end of the war Chrysler Corporation published a small book, *Tanks are Mighty Fine Things*,[19] from which the preceding quotations have been drawn. This book, though in some places as folksy as its title suggests, tells a story of production at the arsenal that is nevertheless heroic.

Other Wartime Projects

The torpedo plant for the Amertorp Corporation was commissioned jointly by the Navy and the American Can Company and was designed in late 1941 and early 1942 (fig. 93). Kahn's comments about the selection of steel sections "most readily obtainable" and the need to consider simplicity of fabrication are pertinent to the design of this plant. Beams are used instead of trusses and are fabricated into rigid bents following the monitor profile and supported at the midpoints of the valleys. Beams were used instead of trusses for two reasons: the smaller sections necessary for trusses were probably assigned to aircraft and ship use, and the choice of solid beam members also reduced the numbers of connections to be fabricated, thus speeding delivery and reducing labor costs. The work in this plant is meticulous, involving small parts in great numbers, and for that reason the monitors are closely spaced. They are 5 feet in vertical dimension and are etched and tinted against sun glare to the south, east, and west. The high roof, 27 feet to the upper ceiling, creates very even light distribution below.

Kahn designed a number of other plants for war matériel. One of these was a propeller works for Curtiss-Wright at Caldwell, New Jersey. Others were generally in the Midwest, between the mountains, because of the Army's fear of air attack.[20] These included the Ford Willow Run plant for B-24 Liberator bombers, the already mentioned Glenn Martin plant at Omaha, an engines factory for Chrysler at Chicago, and a series of plants for Curtiss-Wright in Cincinnati and Columbus, Ohio, and Robertson, Missouri. The best known of the group is Willow Run, but its fame is due to its great size; otherwise, it is not of sufficient interest to merit individual discussion. Typical of his Curtiss-Wright work was the fighter plane factory done in 1941 in Buffalo, New York (figs. 94–98), where Kahn had built the Pierce Plant in 1906. Of all his factories built since the Pierce Plant, this comes closest to it in its planning. The administration unit fronts the street, and the power plant is to the side. Between the power plant and the manufacturing building is the railroad spur. The broad, one-story, monitor-lit manufacturing building is contiguous to the higher assembly building, whose monitors run perpendicular to those of the manufacturing building. It is a mirror image of the Pierce Plant of 35 years earlier. The Curtiss-Wright Plant does exhibit one innovation in planning principles: a tunnel corridor system runs under the entire plant leading to toilet rooms, cafeteria, security rooms, storage and stock rooms, delivery rooms, and other services not directly a part of the production process. Thus, primary and secondary functions, with their respective circulation systems, are separated. This tunnel-basement system can be seen in figure 94 as the series of separate punched windows along part of the base of the building; the trucks at lower left are bringing deliveries to this level. In its general structure and form the plant derives from the work for Glenn Martin but with much reduced spans. The plant produced the Hawk and Helldiver series of fighter planes—some of the Hawk series are seen to the rear of the assembly rooms in figure 96, a photograph taken four months before Pearl Harbor.

"Beautiful Factories"

In this last decade Kahn did very little nonindustrial work. He designed the General Motors Pavilion for the Chicago Century of Progress Exposition of 1933, and when the exposition continued through 1934, he did the Ford building as well. Both were rather slick modernistic efforts in the style of Norman Bel Geddes. Bel Geddes was consultant to the architects of the fair; his avant-garde streamlined style seemed generally appropriate to the futuristic theme but was particularly suited to the image of an auto maker. Kahn's Ford building of 1934 was especially interesting. Its central rotunda (later moved to Dearborn and domed by Buckminster Fuller) was largely a styling effort, but the 564-foot-long Industrial Exhibits Hall used a bent-beam and

Figure 94
Curtiss-Wright Corporation Airport
Plant, Buffalo, New York, 1941;
aerial view of the total plant.
(Photograph by Forster Studio,
courtesy of Albert Kahn Associates.)

Figure 95
Curtiss-Wright Plant; exterior of the manufacturing unit. (Photograph by Geo. A. Ostertag, courtesy of Albert Kahn Associates.)

Figure 96
Curtiss-Wright Plant; exterior of the
assembly unit. (Photograph by
Hedrich-Blessing, courtesy of Albert
Kahn Associates.)

Figure 97
Curtiss-Wright Plant; interior of the assembly unit. (Photograph by Hedrich-Blessing, courtesy of Albert Kahn Associates.)

Figure 98
Curtiss-Wright Plant; the complex
from the airfield. (Photograph by
Geo. A. Ostertag, courtesy of Albert
Kahn Associates.)

monitor roof similar to that of the Amertorp Plant eight years later. Walter Dorwin Teague did some of the Ford exhibits; Jens Jensen was landscape architect. Kahn's work for the exposition was echoed in his association with the General Motors and Ford pavilions for the New York World's Fair of 1939. These buildings occupied a dominant spot at the fair, standing adjacent to each other and just across from the Trylon and Perisphere, but Kahn seems to have had a more minor role in their design. Bel Geddes was credited as designer for the General Motors building, and Teague for Ford. Kahn received second billing in the credits as architect, which suggests that his role was technical rather than artistic.

In 1936 Kahn also designed the relatively simple Saarinen-like Burton Carillon Tower for the University of Michigan, built just north of Hill Auditorium. Occasionally he also designed a house for some important client or old friend. Otherwise his work in this last decade was almost entirely confined to industrial projects. In this same period he also seems to have coined his famous saying that "architecture is ninety per cent business and ten per cent art." This contrasts with his earlier comments about "architectural merit" occurring because of "attractive grouping and external treatment" and further reflects an increased preoccupation with the industrial side of his practice. This intensification of his commitment to factory design may have been in part a matter of choice, though perhaps subconscious choice. This is suggested, for example, by his attitude toward the administration buildings that usually accompanied the factories. Kahn personally spent very little time with them in these last years, leaving them to clichéd formula solutions. Perhaps he was conceding to the stylistic values of the clients in the treatment of administrative units in order to enjoy greater freedom in the design of the factory; or perhaps he was just impatient to get on with the factory unit itself.[21] In any case, it was the factory he cared about, not the administrative unit. Yet the administration buildings clearly offered greater opportunity for conventional monumental elegance, and he could have given his time to them and not to the factory units if he had wanted to do so. This, of course, points up the larger choice as well; he could have emphasized and enlarged the nonindustrial side of his practice if he had

Figure 99
Albert Kahn at the Farm, Walnut Lake, summer of 1938. (Photograph courtesy of Mrs. Barnett Malbin.)

wanted to, since that alternative was almost certainly always open to him to some degree. Apparently, then, during his last years he was doing what he wanted to do.

The tenor of the times supported his emphasis. Factories had never seemed so admirable to the general public as in the late thirties and early forties. In Kahn's beginning years, just after the turn of the century, the birth of the automobile industry and the concurrent birth of industrial architecture as a profession had provided him with great stimulus, while in the twenties the growth of Rouge and related ventures kept him and his firm intensely busy. In each case, but especially in the twenties, his factories received recognition from the industrial world but went largely unnoticed by architects and the public. But in the thirties and forties industry was basking in unprecedented popularity as an apparent panacea for the Great Depression and as an arsenal for the free world. This popularity was a source of further encouragement for Kahn; it also brought him greater public and professional recognition. Some fifteen of his industrial projects were individually written up in architectural journals between 1937 and 1943. The entire issue of *Architectural Forum* for August 1938 was given over to his work, as was the Michigan Society of Architects' *Weekly Bulletin* for December 30, 1941. In 1933 he received a Gold Medal at the International Exposition of Arts and Sciences in Paris; at the same event he was made Chevalier of the Legion of Honor. In 1942 Syracuse University awarded him a doctorate in fine arts; in the same year the American Institute of Architects gave him a special award in architecture and a medal for service to the war effort. There were private satisfactions as well: his daughter Lydia recalls that often at home in the evening, tired after a long day at work but still studying some of the day's problems in his den, he would talk about his "beautiful factories" with unaffected enthusiasm.

His career did not slowly wane but was abruptly terminated. In the midst of intense pressures of early war production, at age seventy-three, he died in Detroit on December 8, 1942.

He really died with his boots on—instantaneously and without ever having acted like a sick person. At the time he died he had been in bed for several weeks, but he saw his family, and some of his office staff, and so far as I was aware, was doing business as usual from his sickbed.[22]

Notes

1. See Automobile Manufacturers Association, *Automobile Facts and Figures* (Detroit), especially the 1939 edition, p. 8.

2. As, for example, Pierce Arrow, Marmon, Du Pont, Duesenberg, Stutz. Even Packard never fully regained its 1920s dominance.

3. The *Aircraft Year Book* for 1936 (New York: The Aeronautical Chamber of Commerce of America, Inc.), 18th annual edition, p. 11.

4. The *Aircraft Year Book* for 1937, 19th annual edition, p. 11.

5. The *Aircraft Year Book* for 1938, 20th annual edition, p. 11.

6. George Nelson, *Industrial Architecture of Albert Kahn* (New York: Architectural Book Publishing Company, 1939), p. 16.

7. Albert Kahn, address to the New York State Association of Architects at Rochester, New York, September 27, 1940. Much of the address is reprinted in *Architectural Forum* 173, No. 6 (December 1940): 501–503.

8. In my own two years of experience with the firm, Sol King, FAIA, president and Director of Architecture, maintained this same frequent contact with the work of individual personnel.

9. Helen Bennett, "Albert Kahn Gives People What They Want," p. 5, original ms for *American Magazine*, prepared in June 1929.

10. Quoted in *Architectural Forum* 173, No. 6 (December 1940): 501.

11. *Architectural Forum* 51, No. 3 (September 1929): 265–272.

12. Ibid.

13. Ibid.

14. In the Assembly Building; 40 feet in the Export Building.

15. See front cover of W. Hawkins Ferry, *The Legacy of Albert Kahn* (Detroit: Detroit Institute of Arts, 1970) and figs. 194 and 195.

16. *Architectural Forum* 173, No. 6 (December 1940): 501.

17. Some work by private industry, however, was for government-use products. Glenn Martin's plants, for example, were privately constructed but intended to produce Army and Navy bombers. Thus even though automobile production declined after 1938, private business had as great a need for Kahn's services as ever.

18. Quoted in Kenneth Reid, *Industrial Buildings* (New York: F. W. Dodge, 1951), p. 258.

19. Wesley Winans Stout, *Tanks are Mighty Fine Things* (Detroit: Chrysler Corporation, 1946), pp. 125–128.

20. This fear was unrealistic. No bomber produced during the war could have made the trip, loaded, from Europe or Asia to the United States, not even from a base in Iceland or Hawaii, if it had come to that. London to Berlin was a horrifying sortie even in 1944. As a maker of bombers, Glenn Martin appreciated this point, which explains why he remained at Baltimore. The other significant exception, of course, was Boeing of Seattle, who, as designer and builder of the Flying Fortress, fully understood all the problems surrounding the question of range.

21. That it was the latter is the strongly held opinion of Sol King, FAIA, president of the current firm, who was project architect in the flourishing late thirties.

22. Letter from Mrs. Butzel to the author, April 10, 1967.

8
AN APPRAISAL

We are now, perhaps, in a position to appraise Kahn's career—to see how he affected the course of architectural history, the ways in which he represented and contributed to an aspect of his time, and some ways in which his innovations may extend beyond the limits of his time to affect the state and condition of his profession.

As already noted, despite the opportunity of continuing a balanced practice, Kahn seems to have chosen to emphasize its industrial side in his last years, only occasionally producing a design that was not a factory. Yet he continued to laud his elegant buildings of earlier days, maintaining to the end that the Clements Library was the design he liked best of anything he had done. This brings us face to face with the dichotomy of Kahn's career: on the one hand, he produced a series of revolutionary, forward-looking, tough-minded industrial solutions; and on the other, he continued to look to a turn-of-the-century, patrician, stylistic elegance. Such seeming contradictions are not unique to Kahn, of course. All men contain them to some degree. An excellent example is Kahn's best client, Henry Ford, who apparently saw no contradiction between a nostalgia for the past of Greenfield Village and a dedication to the Model T, which had made that past irretrievable. And, as we have seen, Edsel Ford, who designed the Lincoln Continental, lived in a "Cotswold" mansion.

In Kahn's case it is possible to suggest some reasons for the dichotomy. In his early years he obviously came to associate professional success in its conventional form with proficiency in period-style elegance. This was natural for a poor boy determinedly ambitious for a profession that to him must have seemed glittering. It is not surprising then that when he achieved professional success, one manifestation of it should take that direction. Nor is it surprising that in later years, when a rather different and highly significant kind of success was overwhelmingly apparent, he would still recall fondly the examples that represented the achievement of that early image. The strength of that image can be measured in part by the degree to which it permeated his other aesthetic perceptions. For just as Henry Ford's nostalgia was accompanied by a certain rejection of history, so Kahn's aesthetic preferences were accompanied by some limitations of aesthetic perception that persisted throughout his life. His meager early philosophic background allowed him to regard practical problems at face value, but in matters involving new or novel aesthetic positions, he did not have the training to deal at necessarily higher levels of philosophic abstraction; and so such novel positions often remained outside his sympathies. This is shown in his lifelong taste for predominantly pre-1870 music and in his taste in the visual arts. His own collection of paintings included a number of first-rate impressionist works, but when his daughter Lydia assembled a more daring collection including the Futurists, Brancusi, and Klee, he confessed he did not understand it. Duchamp, he felt, merited ridicule. He kept in his den an article by an unknown writer entitled "The Farce of Modern Art." In architecture, Wright and Sullivan were to him noble champions of lost causes, well-intentioned but misguided.[1] Kahn also did not understand or enjoy much of the European work. The star performances of European architecture in Kahn's maturity were buildings like Mies van der Rohe's Deutscher Werkbund Pavillion at Barcelona, Gropius's Bauhaus at Dessau, and Le Corbusier's Villa Savoye at Poissy-sur-Seine. Aesthetically these buildings had no links with the past that Kahn could recognize, and he would have seen that they were not straightforward reflections of technical demands since he had consummate experience in that field himself. Thus, they were not comprehensible within either of his frames of reference.

In general, Kahn's clients would have agreed with his viewpoints. There is no doubt that in his aesthetic tastes he received what the psychologist would call strong positive reinforcement from his peers.

It is fair to conclude that if Kahn had produced only nonindustrial work, he would have had only a local interest for the history of architecture. His work in period styles was generally of high quality in its basic elements of proportion and detail and in level of execution, but it lacked the brilliance and vigor of McKim, Mead and White, for example. Kahn, following these men in time, admired them, but their particular milieu and above all their extensive training were not part of his experience. He could approach, not match, their work. With more grooming, perhaps a course of study at the Ecole, he might have carried the McKim banner in slicker style, producing buildings more powerful compositionally in the Ecole sense, as Low Library or Pennsylvania Station (before its demolition) are compositionally powerful. Yet this would have altered his position only to a limited degree. He would have proceeded as far as energy, care, and tasteful emulation could carry him, but he still would have been only one of a crowd, and not the pioneer that in fact he was.

It was because of the factories that he was a unique figure. Here his work was far from being merely tasteful; it was genuinely and boldly inventive. Here his pragmatically innovative mind found its challenge. However, it is necessary to be careful with the record, because the important factories are not necessarily those that have been best known. Neither Packard Plant Number Ten nor Ford Highland Park, interesting as they are, were of primary significance. The Packard building introduced Kahn and the automobile industry to the reinforced-concrete factory, but it was not particularly advanced over other concrete factories for other industries; its reinforcing system was, in fact, less progressive than Ransome's. Ford Highland Park was a beautiful expression of concrete construction and had its day in the sun when, from 1910 to 1913, Ford was using gravity chutes to transfer materials. But Ford's own assembly line meant the end of multistory concrete automobile factories of the Highland Park type. On the other hand, other examples by Kahn can now be seen to have unparalleled significance. The Pierce Plant of 1906 proposed for the first time the one-story roof-lit scheme of unlimited horizontal extension, planned around organized lines of circulation with regard to logically contiguous relationships among various manufacturing processes. Most of its features are found at the Ford Rouge layout fifteen years later; all are found in the Curtiss-Wright plant at Buffalo thirty-five years later. The Packard Forge Shop of 1910 was equally prophetic. It illustrated Kahn's ability to conceive highly original schemes that simultaneously answered problems of structure, light, and ventilation. This inventiveness appeared in fully mature application in the remarkable Ford Rouge Glass Plant of 1922, which also showed that such an innovative scheme could be clad in a thoughtfully simple, efficient envelope. By comparison with any other industrial buildings of their time all of these structures could be properly called revolutionary. The work of Kahn's last decade was a solid culmination of these early efforts. Buildings such as the Chrysler Tank Arsenal show an unequaled ability to transfer to physical form the essence of manufacturing process; the Chrysler Truck Plant and the Glenn Martin Assembly Building represent unequaled ability to develop structure and space in response to general and particular industrial programs; the Glenn Martin addition of 1939 epitomized the smooth rapidity with which these solutions could be put into effect.

Many of the decisions Kahn made in the design of these factories vastly improved the worker's lot. With better light and ventilation he felt more refreshed and was less likely to develop health problems and less prone to injury through accidents. But a reservation already mentioned must be restated. There is not much evidence that these considerations were often ends in themselves. Where they were valued, it was because they improved production. This was illustrated by Henry Ford's comment about better production conditions at Highland Park. The placement of toilets in factories of the thirties, as cited by Moritz Kahn, offers another example: they were closely spaced, not for worker comfort but to minimize travel time. (Would it have been better from a humanistic point of view, and therefore from a perhaps still more enlightened production point of view, to have required of the worker an occasionally longer and perhaps refreshing walk to the facilities?) Corporations of the sort Kahn served do not, of course, exist for purely humanitarian reasons. They exist to make a profit for their stockholders. Given such a purpose, the values imposed in factory design were the only logical ones. The idea that better working conditions make for better production was, in context, both a wise and a civilized realization. Its logical extension into the documented study of architectural conditions that do in fact make for a genuinely happy working situation has not yet been entirely realized. In terms of Kahn's life and work the fairest appraisal is that he was fortunate to work in a time and field in which humanistic concerns were receiving, in the main, increased consideration; and though these humanistic concerns were generally regarded as means, not ends, his designs served them very well—no doubt as well as any architectural devices could have done.

In part, then, Kahn's contributions consist of these architectural artifacts that were of their type. However, he was able to produce them effectively because of his unique what the role of the architect should be—that he should become involved in finding solutions to purely utilitarian design problems. He was willing to grant that such problems could be both significant and challenging, and he took them seriously enough to approach them on their own terms, regarding their requirements without preconceptions. At least equally important are his suggestions for a different architectural design methodology, one in which experts in related fields are not executors but part of the decision-making process from the beginning. More than any other architect of his time, he put this approach into actual practice, showing that it was capable of processing large amounts of data toward a solution of demonstrable usefulness, which could be carried out rapidly. Though the problems he dealt with were fundamentally technical and programmatic in emphasis, humanistic concerns were necessarily a part of these problems and thus of his approach. The timeliness of this attitude needs no elaboration.

In a summation of Kahn's career some comments are in order regarding his reasons for designing the factories in the first place. Some of the reasons are obvious. Success was apparent, and a tidy subsistence went with it. There were impressive fringe benefits as well in the form of related nonindustrial commissions, and here we might note the surprising, even overwhelming, number of commissions that came as a direct or indirect result of industrial contacts. The entire body of work for the University of Michigan was indirectly related; and the Joy residence, the Detroit Athletic Club, the General Motors Building, the Fisher Building, the Edsel Ford home, the Ford World's Fair work, and a number of other buildings as well are obviously directly related. Kahn's career in its entirety was in fact far more closely tied to industry than a simple tabulation of "industrial" and "nonindustrial" works suggests, a point of which Kahn himself could hardly have been unaware. Kahn's factory design tendencies were reinforced by his own personality as well. He must have enjoyed doing the factories; his comments about their design always have a true ring of enthusiasm, and furthermore, men seldom excel at things they do not enjoy. (It could also be argued that men enjoy most those things they do well, but the point remains.) His lack of introspection, of philosophic profundity, the very qualities that limited him at higher levels of abstraction, left him particularly open to suggestions inherent in this new kind of architectural problem. This quality of mind he shared with Henry Ford and others; it was to a degree a necessary characteristic of many pioneers in the industrial burgeoning of the early twentieth century. Kahn also shared with these pioneers concentration and determination, while his seriousness about money matters would have won the hearts and, more importantly, the business minds of most industrialists. But his ability to listen, and thereby to accept information, was in the end the fundamental key to his success. It accounts for his willingness to form a team and to draw fully upon its potential, and it also accounts for his attention to the operational problems of industry.

Kahn lay outside any architectural movement, American or European. In one aspect of his career he belonged to the eclectics, but in another he far outdistanced them. Temperamentally and therefore professionally he was at the opposite pole from the evocative architectural poetry of Wright. Yet he was not related to the Europeans either. Behrens, the Futurists, De Stijl, the Bauhaus, the International Style—all constituted a celebration of machine age potentials at a significantly symbolic level; Kahn's work was an attempt to solve machine age production needs at an almost exclusively operational level. Even the Futurists and the Bauhaus, the most machine-vocal movements, had less to say about program needs than about materials, and less to say about economy than either. Kahn directed his efforts toward satisfying all three needs, as he had to do in a pragmatic rather than a theoretical context, while at the same time he expressed relatively minor concern for conscious formal or symbolic intent. Thus he was able to comprehend and satisfy with unique success the complex needs of industry in a technological age.

It is clear that Kahn was not cut in the mold of the conscious reformer. He believed in the course of events of his time and tried to make his contribution, not by challenging, but by encouraging that course. He believed particularly in that most essential phenomenon of the early twentieth century, the maturation of heavy industry. Early in life he not only had ambitions for architecture but also had grown up in a city charged with the excitement of industry. From 1902 on he was with men—his clients and friends—who were a key part of the phenomenon: Henry Joy, William Durant, the Fisher brothers, Glenn Martin, and, perhaps above all, Ford and his associates. In the company of these men he found his own industrial interests and predilections encouraged. He had a broader source of encouragement as well, because an infatuation with industry was by no means confined to any such closed circle: it was shared by society as a whole. From the individual farmer's appreciation for the liberating efficiency of his tractor to the world's romantic adulation of Lindbergh's flight, society shared and enjoyed the products of industry at a widespread level indeed. The excitement was never unanimous; there were always voices of dissent, but they were few in number. The excitement of the industrializing era was focused on the great boon of the automobile, especially the cheap automobile as exemplified by the Model T; the conclusion of the war to end wars; the utilization of assembly line production; the invention and coming of age of the airplane; and the salvation from the Great Depression provided by manufacturing. In part Kahn was caught up in these events, and they did a great deal to shape his life and career. He shared a widespread excitement as well as a social value system taken for granted by all but the very few. But Kahn was at the frontiers. While the broad sweep of history was directed by underlying social forces, he was operating at its cutting edge, deflecting the path of events, speeding their course through the architectural process.

Kahn left some eminently useful buildings and some very handsome ones. These constitute an important facet of architectural history in their own right. They have had an impact on the world as it is, both through their architectural presence and because of the role they played in encouraging industrialization. Our world today is not Kahn's world, and some of our problems are due to the very industrialization he served. Paradoxically, however, his career also suggests some rays of hope for his profession as it faces the difficulties of a later time. In addition to the buildings, he left a testimony to the significance and the excitement of utilitarian design challenges and to the importance of adhering to precise criteria, and he showed that a genuine team attack on design problems has undeniable usefulness. The potential of these contributions has not yet been fully tested but would appear to extend far beyond the industrial sphere into the broadest spectrum of present design concerns.

Note

1. However, one should not overstate the case here; Kahn's view was no more or less conservative than the prevailing one. Hugh Morrison (*Louis Sullivan, Prophet of Modern Architecture* [New York: Museum of Modern Art and W. W. Norton Co., 1935], p. xviii) notes that a similar attitude prevailed, even among distinguished critics and historians, as late as the early thirties. At that time, of course, Sullivan had been dead for years, while Wright was at his absolute nadir, his career apparently long since finished.

INDEX

(Numerals in boldface refer to illustrations.)

Academic theory, Kahn's lack of, 20–21. *See also* Pragmatism, of Kahn

Acoustics
analysis of, 73
design for, 79

Adler, Dankmar, 16

Adler and Sullivan, office of, 16

Administration buildings, Kahn's attitude toward, 213

A.E.G. Turbinenfabrik, 62–65 passim, 121

Aircraft industry. *See also* Curtiss-Wright Corporation; Glenn L. Martin Assembly Building; Glenn L. Martin Plant
first work for, 126
growth of, 152–153

Airplanes. *See* Curtiss-Wright Corporation; Glenn L. Martin Assembly Building; Glenn L. Martin Plant

Air power, military uses of, 153

Allgemeine Electrizitäts Gesellschaft. *See* A. E. G. Turbinenfabrik

American Architect, 54, 150–151

American Architect and Building News, Travelling Scholarship of, 9

American Institute of Architects, award from, 214

Amertorp Torpedo Plant, **204**, 205, 213

Amtorg Trading Corporation, 128

Anderson, Stanford, 63, 65

Angell Hall at University of Michigan, 135, **141**

Architect, role of, 2, 3, 221

Architectural design, methodology for, 221. *See also* Self-sufficiency, of Kahn office

Architectural Forum, 214

Architectural League, Silver Medal of, 151

"Architectural Trend," in *Journal of the Maryland Academy of Sciences*, 18

Army-Navy "E" award, for production excellence, 203

Asbestos metal, use of, 99

Assembly line
effect on Kahn office of, 164
impact of, 91–92, 223
and plant design, 39, 43, 120
at Rouge complex, 122

Austin Company, use of sawtooth systems by, 108

Automobile industry. *See also* Ford, Henry; Ford Highland Park Plant; Model T; Packard Plant Number Ten; Pierce Plant
assembly in, 51
birth of, 214
Detroit as center of, 22, 27–28
effect of Depression on, 152
Kahn's first work for, 27

Bacon, Henry, influence of, 9, 14

Ballinger Company, industrial architecture of, 109

Ballinger Super-Span system, 109, 111

Banham, Reyner, 63, 109

Barcelona Pavilion. *See* Deutscher Werkbund Pavillon, Barcelona

Bates Manufacturing Company, 55
factory for, 59

Bauhaus, 218, 222

"B" Building. *See* Ford Eagle Plant

Beams, instead of trusses, 205

Behrens, Peter, 2, 64, 121, 222
and aesthetic composition, 65, 66
work of, 62–63

Bel Geddes, Norman, 206, 213

Benyon, Marshall and Bage Flax Mill, at Shrewsbury, England, 31

Benz, Karl, 6

Bessemer converter, 5

Bessemer steel, 22

Boats, mass production of, 92, 93. *See also* Ford Rouge Complex

Bogardus, James, 31

Boyer, Joseph, 25, 26

Brancusi, Constantin, 218

Brick, use of, 73, 79, 80

Bridge construction, ideas from, 183, 184, 194

Briscoe brothers, 27

Broad Street Station, Philadelphia, 183

Bruges, sketch of, **12**

B-24 Liberator bombers, plant for, 215

B-26 Marauder, plant for, 197

Burnham, D. H., 31, 133

Burroughs Adding Machine Company, 92

Burton Carillon Tower, University of Michigan, 213

Butler Art Institute, 135

Caldwell, Charles, 31, 33

Cantilevering, 173, 182, 194

Chalmers Motor Company, 55, 124

Chapin, Roy, 27

Chelyabinsk, USSR, tractor plant at, 128, 129

Chevrolet Commercial Body Plant, 157–165, **159–163**

Chicago, architectural movement in, 20

Chicago and Alton Railroad Bridge, 183

Chicago Century of Progress Exposition, designs for, 206, 213

Chicago Tribune Tower, 147, 150

Children's Hospital, Detroit, 25

Chrysler Corporation
De Soto Press Shop of (see De Soto Press Shop)
effect of Depression on, 152
Engineering Building of, 124

Chrysler Half-Ton Truck Plant, 172–183, **176–181**

Chrysler Tank Arsenal, 197–205, **199–203**

Churchill, Winston, 203

Circulation matrix
in Curtiss-Wright Plant, 206
at Ford Highland Park Plant, 120
at Ford Rouge Plant, 120
at Krupp complex, 122
at Pierce Plant, 39, 219

Cité Industrielle, 61, 62

Civil engineering, ideas from, 198

Clements Memorial Library, University of Michigan, 135, **140**, 217

Clients, analysis of, 86

Coignet, François, 32

Columbia University, Low Library at, 82, 219

Conservatism, of nonindustrial work, 86

Continental Motor Car Company, 55

Contributions, of Kahn, 221, 224

Cotswold Hills, architecture of, 146

Cranbrook Academy of Art, 150

Cranbrook House, Bloomfield Hills, 72

Craneway, 62
in Ford Glass Plant, 108
in Packard Forge Shop, 54

Cret, Paul Phillipe, 20, 21

Crucible Steel Company mill, 183

Curtiss-Wright Corporation
fighter plane plant for, 206, **207–211**, 219
propeller works for, 205
Stack Shops and Storage Building for, 172, **174**, **175**, 203

Daimler, Gottlieb, 6

Depression, effect on industry of, 128, 152, 223

De Soto Press Shop, 165, **166–171**

De Stijl, 222

Detroit
as automobile center, 22, 27–28
Kahn's early days in, 6–7, 22–23

Detroit Athletic Club, 26, 80–85, **81, 83–85,** 221

Detroit Free Press Building, 87

Detroit Golf Club, 26, 72

Deutscher Werkbund Pavillon, Barcelona, 218

Dill, Sir John, 205

Dime Bank Building, Detroit, 133

Dinamismo Architettonico, 65

D. M. Ferry Seed Company, 22

Dodge, Horace, 27, 55

Dodge, John, 27, 55

Dodge plant, description of, 59

Duchamp, Marcel, 218

Durant, William, 223

Eagle Plant. See Ford Eagle Plant

Echternach, Luxembourg, 5, 6, 22

Ecole des Beaux-Arts, 9, 20, 219
influence of, 21, 61

Economics, Kahn's approach to, 3, 7, 21

Economy. See also Efficiency; Kahn office; Self-sufficiency
of Chevrolet Commercial Body Plant design, 164
in design, 72, 87
at Ford Glass Plant, 109
value in, 16

Edmunds, Henry E., 120

Efficiency. See also Economy; Self-sufficiency
in Amertorp Torpedo Plant, 205
through assembly lines, 91
in Chrysler Tank Arsenal design, 203, 205
of construction, 164
of Kahn office, 156, 193–194, 197 (see also Kahn office)
at Krupp complex, 122
of truss-monitor scheme, 165, 172
in Soviet plants, 130
through steel construction, 99

Elevators, 91

Engineering Building, University of Michigan, 26, 27, 72

Envelope
of Chrysler Half-Ton Truck Plant, 172
efficient, 122
of Ford Motor Assembly Building, 117
of Ford Rouge Glass Plant, 219
and structure, 183

Essen, Germany, 5, 121, 122

227
Index

European scholarship travel, 9–14, **10–13**
Expansion, provision for, 122, 182,
E-Z Shoe Polish factory, 61, 64

Factories. *See also* Industry; Industrial architecture
aesthetic merit of, 65
early English, 31
public approval of, 214
role of, 1, 2
steel-framed, 31
as symbol, 63, 67, 222
Fagus Shoe-last Factory, 63
"Farm," The. *See* Walnut Lake house
Fiat, factory for, 109
Fischer Marble Company, steel structure for, 31
Fisher, Fred J., 27
and brothers, 223
Fisher Body Corporation, factory for, 124
Fisher Building, 2, 147–151, **148–149**, 221
Flat span, 183, 184
Flexibility, in design, 39, 122, 198
Ford, Edsel, 217
home of, 146–147, 221
Ford, Henry, 19, 27, 164, 222
and assembly line, 91
as client, 86
and Eagle Plant, 92–93
early manufacturing methods of, 45, 51
and Glass Plant, 101
growth theories of, 117, 120
influence of, 223
inventiveness of, 126

labor policies of, 123
and one-story scheme, 99
personality of, 43–44, 217
self-sufficiency goal of, 100, 111, 112, 128
as team leader, 127
on work conditions, 52, 53, 220
Ford By-products Plant, 111
Ford Cement Plant, 111
Ford Coke Ovens, **110**, 111
Ford Eagle Plant, 92–99, **94–98**
Ford Educational Department, on work conditions, 53
Ford Engineering Laboratory
bent beams in, 173
interior of, 124, **125**
roof of, 126
Ford Glass Plant, 110–111, **103–107**
significance of, 111, 219, 220
ventilation in, 102, 108, 123
windows in, 117
Ford Highland Park Plant, 43–54, **46–50**
air distribution in, 124
assembly line in, 91
circulation matrix of, 120
and Fiat factory, 109
ornamentation on, 59
replacement of, 100
significance of, 45, 51, 219
use of steel at, 92
Ford Job Foundry, 111
Ford Motor Assembly Building, 111, **118, 119**
envelope treatment at, 117
Ford Motor Company
branch plants for, 124
effects of Depression on, 152
founding of, 27

job records of, 60
Soviet connections of, 129–130
teamwork at, 127
Ford Motor Company Plant. *See* Ford Highland Park Plant; Ford Rouge Complex
Ford Motor Company Service Building, 87
Ford Open Hearth Building, **110**, 111–117, **113–116**
ventilation in, 123
Ford Pavilion, at New York World's Fair, 213
Ford Piquette Plant, manufacturing methods at, 45
Ford Power House, **110**
Ford Pressed Steel Building, **110**, 111
Ford Rolling Mill, **110**
Ford Rouge Complex, 1, **110**, 118, 219. *See also* Ford Eagle Plant; Ford Glass Plant; Ford Motor Assembly Building; Ford Open Hearth Building
beginnings of, 92–100
expansion of, 100–120, 214
significance of, 121–123
Ford Spring and Upset Building, **110**, 111
Ford Willow Run Plant, 205
Formulated approach, advantages of, 164, 197
for Chevrolet Plant, 157–163
for De Soto Press Shop, 165
Franco-Prussian War, of 1870–1871, 5
Free Press Building, Detroit, 150
Freer house, **15**, 72, 87
vitality of, 83

Fuller, Buckminster, 206
Furnaces
  in Ford Glass Plant, 108
  in Open Hearth Building, 112
Futurists, 22, 23, 218, 222
  theories of, 65–66, 67

Garnier, Tony, 20, 61, 62, 66
Garrick Theatre, 73
General Motors Building, 2, 133–
  135, **136–139**
General Motors Corporation, effect
  of Depression on, 152
General Motors Pavilion
  at Chicago Exposition, 206
  at New York World's Fair, 213
Getty Tomb, 73
Gilbert, Cass, 133
Glass. See also Lighting, natural
  in Fagus Shoe-last Factory, 63, 64
  Kahn's use of, 29, 52
  for Model Ts, 100
  production of, 101 (see also Ford
  Glass Plant)
  Ransome's use of, 33
Glass Plant. See Ford Glass Plant
Glenn L. Martin Assembly Build-
  ing, 183–193, **185–192**
Glenn L. Martin Plant, 117, 126, 185,
  195
  addition to, 193–197, **196,** 205, 220
  Administration Building of, **189**
Goodrich, B. F., Rubber Company,
  55
Grace Hospital Nurse's Home, 25
Gravity chutes, 45, 52, 219
Gray, Edward, 52
Gropius, Walter, 2, 63
  and aesthetic composition, 65, 66, 67

architecture of, 63–64
and Ecole theory, 20
factory interests of, 121
Kahn's opinion of, 218
team concept of, 155
Gunite, use of, 117, 158, 165

Hawk fighter planes, production of,
  206
Helldiver fighter planes, produc-
  tion of, 206
Hennebique, François, 32, 33
Hicks, Sir Baptist, 146
Highland Park Plant. See Ford
  Highland Park Plant
Hill Memorial Auditorium, Uni-
  versity of Michigan, 18, 73–79,
  75–78, 83, 86
Historic precedent, Ecole theory of,
  20
Hitler, Adolf, rearmament plans
  of, 153
Holt house, 72
Hudson Motor Car Company, 55
Hudson plant, 57, 59
Humanistic considerations, of
  Kahn's designs, 55, 220, 221. See
  also Work conditions
Humanistic contributions, of Rouge
  Complex, 123. See also Work
  conditions
Hunt, Richard Morris, 14, 20
Hyatt, Thaddeus, 32

Industrial architecture. See also
  Factories
  birth of, 214
  Depression's effect on, 128

development of, 34
European, 61–67, 109, 121–122
history of, 31–33
Industrial Exhibits Hall, 206
Industrial Works factory, 55, 59
International Exposition of Arts
  and Sciences, awards from, 214
Iron, disadvantages of, 31–32
Italy, Kahn's visit to, 80, 82

Jensen, Jens, 213
Journal of the Royal Institute of
  British Architects, on industrial
  architecture, 109
Joy, Henry B., 26, 27, 28
  influence of, 80, 223
  residence of, 72, **74,** 87, 221
Joy, James, 26
Joy house. See Joy, Henry B., resi-
  dence of

Kahn, Albert. See also Kahn office
  culminating work of, 152–216
  death of, 214–215
  education of, 6, 19, 20, 44
  homes of, 7, 72, 87–88
  marriage of, 16–17, 18, 23
  as office manager, 154–157
  personality of, 21–22, 218, 222
  popular recognition of, 214
  pragmatism of, 3, 19, 21, 34, 61, 64,
    65, 219, 222
  and Soviet commission, 128–130
Kahn, Edgar (son), 90
Kahn, Ernestine Krolik (wife), 80,
  89
  courtship of, 16, 17, 18, 23
  influence of, 19
Kahn, Joseph (father), 5, 6, 7

Kahn, Julius (brother), role of, 26, 29, 59. *See also* Trussed Concrete Steel Company; "Kahn System of Reinforced Concrete"

Kahn, Louis (brother), 59, 153

Kahn, Lydia (daughter), 214, 218

Kahn, Mollie (sister), 17

Kahn, Moritz (brother), 100, 158, 220

administration of, 153

on formulated approach, 157, 164

on Kahn office structure, 127–128

on process organization, 101

Soviet trip of, 129

Kahn, Rosalie (daughter), 89

Kahn, Rosalie (mother), 5, 7

Kahn bar. *See* "Kahn System of Reinforced Concrete"

Kahn office. *See also* Kahn, Albert growth of, 100, 126, 153, 197

organization of, 60, 127–128, 153–155

self-sufficiency of, 154, 164, 193, 194, 197

team concept in, 127, 155, 156–157, 224

"Kahn System of Reinforced Concrete," 29, 33

Kanzler, Ernest, 91

King, Charles, 27, 28

Kirkaldy, David, 32

Klann, William C., 123

Klee, Paul, 218

Knudsen, William S., 198

Koenen, K., 32

Kresge Building, 87

Krolik, Ernestine. *See* Kahn, Ernestine Krolik

Krupp complex, 5, 121–122

Krupp family, 5, 6

Krupp guns, assembly of, 121

Kuznetsk, USSR, plants at, 129

Labor relations, deterioration of, 123. *See also* Work conditions; Workers, contentment of

Lambot, Joseph, 32

Larchmont Manor, 17

Le Corbusier, 20, 121, 218

Lee, Gilbert W., residence of, 8

Leland, Henry M., 27

Light, distribution of, 108, 205. *See also* Lighting

Lighting, natural,

in A. E. G. Turbinenfabrik, 62

in Amertorp Torpedo Plant, 205

in Chrysler Half-Ton Truck Plant, 173

in Chrysler Tank Arsenal, 203

in Curtiss-Wright Stack Shops and Storage Building, 172

in early English factories, 31

in Ford Eagle Plant, 93

in Ford Glass Plant, 102, 108, 117

in Ford Highland Park Plant, 52, 53, 54

in Ford Motor Assembly Building, 117

in Ford Open Harth Building, 112

in Ford Rouge complex, 123

in General Motors Building, 135

in Glenn L. Martin Assembly Building, 184

in Krupp complex, 122

in Packard Forge Shop, 55, 66

in Packard Plant Number Ten, 33

in Pierce Plant, **37**, 38, 39

in Walnut Lake house, 87, 89

Lincoln Memorial, 9

Lincoln Motor Company, steel-framed addition to, 124

Lindbergh, Charles A., 152

Lockwood, Green and Company, 34, 35

Loire, châteaux of, 14

Low Library, Columbia University, 82, 219

Lozier Motor Company, 55

Luxembourg, Kahn's scholarship visit to, 9, 14. *See also* Echternach, Luxembourg

Maccabees Building, 150

McCauley, Alvan, 147

MacDonald, William, 193

McKim, Charles Follen, influence of, 18, 19, 20, 73, 86

McKim, Mead, and White, work of, 21, 73, 80, 82, 83, 135, 218

Mack Printing Company, 55

McMillan, James, 25

Marinetti, Filippo, 65

Marquette Building, Kahn's offices in, 60

Marquis, Samuel, 123

Martin, Glenn L., 126, 183, 193, 223

Martin Assembly Building. *See* Glenn L. Martin Assembly Building

Mason, George D., 8, 13, 17, 25

Mason and Rice, Kahn's early training at, 7–8, 19

Mass production, and assembly line, 91

Matté-Trucco, Giaccomo, 109

Maxwell, John, 27

Maxwell Motor Company plant, additions to, 124

Melchers, Julius, 7, 8

Mendelsohn, Eric, 66

Messel, Alfred, 62

Metropolitan Club, 18

Meyer, Adolph, 63, 64

M4 Sherman tanks, production of, 203

Michigan Central Depot, Detroit, 22

Michigan Society of Architects, *Weekly Bulletin* of, 214

Mies van der Rohe, Ludwig, 218

Model T. *See also* Automobile industry; Ford, Henry
factory production of, 43, 44, 100 (*see also* Ford Highland Park Plant)
obsolescence of, 117
popularity of, 51, 223

Moholy-Nagy, Laszlo, factory interests of, 121

Monier, Josef, 32

M3 General Grant tank, production of, 198, 203

Multistory scheme. *See also* One-story scheme
abandonment of, 51, 152, 219
and concrete, 92, 109
at Ford Highland Park plant, 45, 91, 219

National Bank Building, 135

National Theatre, 87

Nettleton, George, 18, 25

Nettleton and Kahn, commissions of, 25

Nettleton, Kahn and Trowbridge,

practice of, 18, 25

Nevins, Allan, 53, 123, 127

New York World's Fair, Kahn's connection with, 213

Newberry Women's Residence, University of Michigan, 27

New Center Building, Detroit, 151

Niagara Falls, Kahn's visit to, 17

Ohio Steel Foundry, 182–183

Olds, Ransom E., contribution of, 27

Oldsmobiles, first production of, 27

Olds Motor Works, in Detroit, 27

One-story scheme. *See also* Multistory scheme
Ford's commitment to, 91, 99
and steel framing, 92

Open Hearth Building. *See* Ford Open Hearth Building

Ornamentation
of General Motors Building, 133
of Hill Memorial Auditorium, 73
by Wilby, 59

Owatonna Bank, 73

Pacific Coast Borax Company, plant of, 33

Packard, James Ward, 28

Packard factory. *See* Packard Motor Car Company

Packard Forge Shop, 54–55, **56–58,** 86, 92, 219

Packard Motor Car Company, 27, 28, 54
during Depression, 152

Packard Plant Building Number Ten, 28–34, **30**
compared to Ford Highland Park

Building, 44–45
compared to Pierce Plant, 39
importance of, 34, 219
reputation of, 43

Paige Motor Company, 100

Palmer Building, 87

Parke, Davis and Company, factory of, 22

PBM Mariner, assembly of, 193

PB2M Mars, assembly of, 193

Pennsylvania Station, New York, 219

Perret, Auguste, 20, 62

Pershing tanks, production of, 203

Personal Space, 54

Photographs, taken by Kahn, **142, 143, 144**

Piazza San Marco, **81**

Pierce, George N., Company, 35
and economy, 109

Pierce Plant, 34–43, **36–37, 40–42**
building relationships of, 122
compared to Curtiss-Wright Plant, 206
importance of, 34, 39, 101, 219
as prototype, 120, 219

Piquette Plant, manufacturing methods at, 45

Plymouth Motor Corporation
effect of Depression on, 152
plant for, 124

Police Headquarters, Detroit, 135

Post, Wiley, 152

Pragmatism, of Kahn, 3, 19, 21, 34, 61, 64, 65, 219, 222. *See also* Efficiency

Process organization, determination of, 101, 154

Pullman Company Plant, 22

Railroad platform, in Chrysler Half-Ton Truck Plant, 182

Railroad spur, in Chrysler Tank Arsenal, 198, **199**

Railroad tracks, for transport of materials, 93, 111

Ransome, Ernest, reinforced concrete work of, 32–34

Reinforced concrete
advantages of, 91–92
construction with, 26, 28, 29, 31, 43, 109, 219
in Ford Highland Park Plant, 44–45
history of, 32–33
in Packard Plant, 28–29, 33
in Pierce Plant, 38

Rhaunen, Germany, 5

Richardson, Henry Hobson, 7, 14, 17, 18, 19

Roof
bent beam and monitor, 213
of Chrysler Half-Ton Truck Plant, 173
in Fagus Shoe-last Factory, 64
of Ford Open Hearth Building, 117
iron, 31
monitor system on (*see* Lighting, natural)
sawtooth, 108, 109, 121

Roofing, cement tile, 93

Rouge River, as site, 92

Rouge River Complex. *See* Ford Rouge Complex

Ruhr Valley, heavy industry in, 5, 6

Saarinen, Eliel, 147, 150, 213

St. Ambrogio, Milan, 142, **145**, 146

St. Pierre, Caen, France, 9, **13**

Sant'Elia, Antonio, 65, 66

Schuster, Rudolph, 32

Scott and Company, architectural firm of, 7

Scripps, James E., library for, 25

Self-sufficiency
Ford's views on, 100, 111, 112, 128
of Kahn office, 154, 164, 193, 194, 197

Shingle style, 7

Simplicity. *See also* Economy; Efficiency
of construction, 197, 205
of Kahn's composition, 72, 87

Sommer, Robert, 54

Sorenson, Charles, 123

Speed, in factory construction, 43, 164, 193–194, 203, 205

Stalingrad, plants at, 129

Standardization, in Kahn office. *See* Formulated approach

Steam locomotives, as symbol, 22

Steel. *See also* One-story scheme; Reinforced concrete, construction with
advantages of, 92
continuous production of, 111
disadvantages of, 31–32
efficiency of, 99
first use in factories of, 31
Kahn's use of, 54, 111, 122

Stirrup reinforcing, 32

Studebaker Corporation, factory for, 124

Sullivan, Louis, 16
influence of, 19–20, 73, 218
skyscrapers of, 31
Transportation Building of, 18

Swift, Charles, house of, 146

Syracuse University, honorary doctorate from, 214

Tallant, Hugh, 73

Tanks, production of, 198, 203, 205. *See also* Chrysler Tank Arsenal

Tanks are Mighty Fine Things, 205

Teague, Walter Dorwin, 213

Team concept
advantages of, 165, 224
in Kahn office, 127, 155–156

Team work, Kahn's ability at, 26, 154–155, 222

Thermal expansion, 32

Toilet rooms, provision for, 158, 220

Trowbridge, Alexander B., 18, 25

Truss
Pratt, 158, 203
simple span, 165, 172
Warren, 194

Trussed Concrete Building, 59, 87

Trussed Concrete Steel Company. *See also* Kahn, Julius
formation of, 26
and Packard Plant Building Number Ten, 29
and Pierce Plant, 34

Trusses
in Ballinger Super Span System, 109–111
in Chevrolet Commercial Body Plant, 157–158
in Chrysler Half-Ton Truck Plant, 173, 182
in Chrysler Tank Arsenal, 203
in Curtiss-Wright Stack Building, 172
in De Soto Press Shop, 165
in Ford Eagle Plant, 93, 99

in Ford Glass Plant, 102, 108
framing monitors, 108
in Glenn L. Martin Assembly
  Building, 184
Tunnel corridor system, 206

University Club, New York, 82
University of Michigan
  Angell Hall of, 135, 141
  Burton Carillon Tower of, 213
  Clements Library of, 135, **140, 141,**
    217
  Delta Upsilon fraternity of, 72
  Engineering Building of, 26, 27, 72
  General Library of, 79
  Hill Memorial Auditorium of, 73
  Newberry Women's Residence of,
    27
  Science Building of, 79
United Shoe Machine Company, 33
U.S. Aviation School, 80
USSR, commission from, 128–130

Van Rensselaer, Marianna G., 17, 19
Ventilation
  in Ford Glass Plant, 102, 108, 123
  in Ford Highland Park Plant, 52,
    124
  in Ford Open Hearth Building,
    112, 123
  in Packard Forge Shop, 55, 66
  in Pierce Plant, 38
Vesnin, V. A., 129
Vibration, damping of, 92
Vignola, Giacomo, 135, 142
Villa Savoye, 218
Vitré, sketch of, **11**

Walker, Chandler, house of, 146

Walker, Hiram, 25
Walker, R. T., on Rouge complex,
  117
Walnut Lake house, 7, 87–90, **88**
Ward, William E., house of, 32
Wayss, E. A., 32
Wilby, Ernest
  and Hill Memorial Auditorium, 73
  ornamentation by, 64
  partnership with, 25–26
  role of, 59
Williams-Ellis, Clough, 128
Wind loads, countering of, 112
Woolworth Building, 133
Work circulation, at Pierce Plant,
  39. *See also* Circulation matrix
Work conditions. *See also* Humanis-
  tic considerations; Labor relations
  at Ford Highland Park Plant, 53–
  54
  improvement of, 52–53
  Kahn's concern with, 55
Workers, contentment of, 53, 123,
  220. *See also* Humanistic considerations; Work conditions
Work process, at Piquette plant, 45
World War I, effect on industry of,
  223
World War II, effect on industry of,
  197–206
Wright, Frank Lloyd, 16
  comparison of Kahn with, 222
  E-Z Shoe Polish Factory of, 64
  influence of, 18, 19, 87, 218
  Soviet tour of, 128
  technological interests of, 61
Wyandotte, Michigan, 22